A WOMAN'S FEAR
FEMALE ABUSE

From Best Selling Author
CAESAR RONDINA

authorHOUSE®

AuthorHouse™
1663 Liberty Drive
Bloomington, IN 47403
www.authorhouse.com
Phone: 1 (800) 839-8640

Published by AuthorHouse 12/04/2018

ISBN: 978-1-5462-7154-3 (sc)
ISBN: 978-1-5462-7152-9 (hc)
ISBN: 978-1-5462-7153-6 (e)

Library of Congress Control Number: 2018914494

The topics discussed in this book are not a reflection of the opinion of the author. The topics in this book are based on facts, research, and the author's real-life experience, and true stories told by those affected. No references will ever be made to names or locations. The privacy of any individual is fully protected.

ALSO BY CAESAR RONDINA

The Warrior Within
Making Partnership Choices
Balancing The Scale
Who Are The Heroes
The Soul In Our Hearts
Best Selling Author of
Management and Employee Relations
(now available as a tutorial at udemy.com)
Leadership Skills for Success

www.caesarrondinaauthor.com Twitter - @ caesarrondina Facebook - Caesar Rondina Author

CONTENTS

CONTENTS

DEDICATION

This book is dedicated to every woman who has suffered from abuse in any form and shared her stories in this book. It is a woman's greatest fear. For the victim, it can leave both physical and emotional scars for a long time. Scars that need time to heal. Some may, and others may not. However, they can be dealt with. I applaud every woman for their tenacity, strength, and courage to overcome those fears.

INTRODUCTION

Before we start, I would like to state, *at no time in this book will any names or locations be used. The privacy of those who were willing to share their stories and the oath I took as a paramedic and firefighter will be respected.* This book is not only about true stories and reality. It is about prevention and awareness. What is abuse? Abuse is a demon that can sneak up on you without warning. Abuse is something no woman expects, and no woman is prepared for. It is a deep routed fear in the sub-conscious of someone's mind. Something that is always there, but not thought of until it happens. If it does, it can be a life-altering and devastating experience. You do not know why, nor do you understand it. Honestly, you never will. However, to heal, you need to accept what happened and take steps to ensure it NEVER happens again. In the vast majority of cases, it is not your fault. Now do not get me wrong. Some women deliberately push someone's buttons. Not everyone is like you. With that said, there is no reason for abuse to occur. A man being abused by a woman is different from a woman being abused by a man. In the vast majority of those cases, it is emotional abuse, not physical abuse. However, in the majority of cases when a woman is abused by a man, it involves some form of physical abuse. I was in an emotionally abusive relationship with a woman. I choose to leave and walk away.

This book offers a great deal of information on this subject as well as referring to actual cases and events I was involved with during my over 30 years as a paramedic. I have also added true stories that have been told to me by women who have experienced abuse. What you take from this book is entirely up to you. One of the things we do as people is shut down when we are hurt. I am involved with volunteering and speak on this topic. Women shut down for many reasons. Reasons we will discuss. The purpose of support groups is to help women face what has happened so they can heal and move forward. As a single man who dates, I have met women that cannot let it go. Therefore, they never move on. No matter how many times they try, many women do not seek help. Do not be that woman. You owe yourself more, which I will demonstrate in this book. As you read along, never lose sight of the fact that there is never a reason for any woman to be abused by a man. Whether provoked or he is a sick human being, he should always walk away.

CHAPTER 1

WHAT IS ABUSE?

I can sit here and write you the dictionary definition for abuse. I will not waste your time or mine. Frankly, it is so vague it can never encompass all the underlying factors. The word "Abuse" is not a one size fits all definition. Simply put, abuse is anything that an individual feels is abusive to them as a person. That will vary from person to person. What might seem abusive to one woman may not be abusive to another. This is due to a variety of reasons. A woman raised in a household where her mother experienced some form of abuse, may not be as sensitive to it, or, she could be mentally hiding from the truth. Anything a person experiences, while they are growing, can have two consequences. First, they may turn out to be the same way, or they may have hated it so much they never want to be like that. I have spoken to women that were raised in an abusive environment that thought it was not only normal but also acceptable. Over time, to that child, this became a learned and accepted behavior. Abuse could also relate to cultural differences. People must remember. There are many cultures. Each has their different beliefs, and many are based around their faith. They all share the same space. However, not all cultures believe the same way. It can also be due to the social environment some experienced. As I stated, I worked over thirty years as a paramedic in a large metropolitan city that also had an inner-city structure. At one time, this city was listed on the FBI top ten list of dangerous cities. I have seen domestic violence in every form, and in every type of neighborhood. It is NOT limited to lower income brackets, or what some people refer to, a word I dislike; "Minorities."

Minority is a demeaning word. It assigns a perceived label on people. Female abuse is not limited to income, race, color, creed, social status, or neighborhood. It happens everywhere. I have seen women attempt suicide because they cannot accept what

1

happened to them, or is happening to them. I have cared for many rape victims. I have seen women brutally beaten to the point that you could not recognize them against their own picture. This is real. It exists. I hope that you have never been a victim of any form of abuse. If you were, you understand. This is an emotionally crippling experience. It demeans a person and strips them of their self-respect. To some people in our society, it slaps a label on them. For every prosecuting attorney, there are more defense attorneys. The job of a defense attorney is to get someone off or get them the best plea bargain deal they can if they are guilty. As with any defense, they will try to show that the woman provoked it, or as it is said, "Asked for it." This may be attempted using what style of clothing she was wearing, her actions, or words. You may hold that against them, but that is their job. It is the main reason many cases of sexual assault are not reported.

The sad truth is, the Criminal Justice System reports that out of 627 reported cases, 255 lead to an arrest, and 105 cases are referred to a prosecutor. Forty-one cases will lead to a felony conviction, and only 33 criminals will be incarcerated. Here is the website to those figures, and more shocking data. *https://www.rainn.org/statistics/criminal-justice-system.* We will be discussing more on this later.

Let me share my first story with you. I had a call where I responded to a 19-year-old female that was beaten and possibly raped. As it turns out, witnesses at the scene reported that they thought she had just started dating someone who was a member of a gang. They claimed they knew nothing more. Although DNA testing today has become much more accurate, many arguments in rape cases are still made as to whether or not the samples are reliable, especially in a case where there were more than one attackers. Also, assailants have gotten smart. Many now wear gloves, masks, and condoms, thus reducing the risk of obtaining DNS samples. In the Colorado serial rapist case against Marc O'Leary, who committed several sexual assaults in multiple jurisdictions, he ordered women to shower, brush their teeth, and he took the bedding and clothing with him. Other things eventually led to his arrest, which connected him to the crime scenes. A book

"An Unbelievable Story of Rape" was written about this case. Going back to my story, the police arrived on scene first, and found a beaten, trembling 19-year-old girl that had no clothes on. They promptly covered her. When we arrived, she was frightened and shaking. She would not let us near her. My partner and I were both men. We called to see if there was a female crew available. There was not. We had to make this work. She was badly beaten and bleeding from her vaginal area. We needed to assess her for any possible life-threatening injuries, and treat her if possible, while maintaining any evidence for the hospital to perform a rape crisis kit. We needed to be sure the police would not have evidence that was contaminated.

In a case like this, the last thing you want to do is force the patient, restrain her, or do anything that could traumatize her further. A female officer arrived. Being the only paramedic on the scene, I had the highest medical authority, so this was my case. I hope a female officer would be able to talk to her and calm her down. She could not. In this short time, her eyes had become very swollen, her lip was cut quite deep and bleeding, and I had no idea of the extent of her vaginal injury. I knew she would never allow me to examine her. I needed to obtain her vital signs to be sure she was stable. The other choice was to provide no care and get her straight to the hospital. At this point, I would take it either way. However, she was so traumatized she would not let anyone near her for us to move her to our stretcher and transport her. The police had found her pocketbook and her ID. Her parents were called and on the way. If we were still there when they got there, this would make the situation even worse. The police told them to go straight to the hospital, but they already knew where she had been found, and she had not been transported yet. If her parents arrived on the scene, those additional emotions could be disastrous. Emotionally, this is the most critical time for a patient. They are sitting on an emotional fence. If they fall to the wrong side, their emotional state can become far worse. We needed to do something. Having a counselor transported to the scene would take too long, or having a female nurse brought to the scene would also take too long. We needed to act quickly.

3

By this time, there were many additional resources on the scene. Our supervisor, detectives, more police, crime scene investigators, and now reporters were starting to show up. This made it much worse for her. I could not begin to imagine how embarrassed she must have been feeling. I thought that might be the problem. All the voices, all the people trying to talk to her, all the noise, was probably scaring her more. I spoke with the police sergeant at the scene. She was a great woman and officer. It was clear she was upset over this as well. I asked to have everyone removed except for her and me so we could have some privacy. I explained what I thought was going on. The people, the voices, and the noise were probably causing her to relive the event. She agreed. She ordered everyone back, and to remain silent. No reporter was ever close enough to take pictures. The officer kneeled near the young girls head, and I sat on the ground about two feet from her face. It was quite. In a very soft voice, I explained that we had everyone leave. It was just her, the female officer, and I. She said, "Thank you." Once she spoke, I knew I had a chance. This was a window of opportunity to gain some trust. These windows are very short, and you must act on them. I told her my name and explained I was there to help her. I explained that I would respect her privacy and had no intentions of making her feel uncomfortable. I told her I would explain everything I was going to do before I did it, and would not do anything she did not want me to do. I also told her the female officer would come with us in the back of the ambulance to the hospital. I wanted no surprises. She asked, "You won't hurt me?" I actually had a tear running down my face, and replied, "I won't let anyone hurt you." Out from under the blanket she put out her hand. It was scrapped and had some blood on it. I explained while putting on a glove that I was wearing the glove because I did not know if the blood on her hands was hers or one of her assailants and did not want to contaminate any evidence.

I took her hand and said, "I will help you." By this time, a female ambulance crew became available and arrived on the scene. They were going to take over her care. When they came over to us, the young girl pulled her hand away from mine, put it under the blanket, and asked, "Why are they here?" I explained I thought she might be more comfortable going to the hospital with a female

crew. She replied, "I want to go with you." I had gained her trust.
I released the other crew, and we moved her into our ambulance. I
kept the backlights off as we drove away so no one could try to get
a picture, even though it had privacy glass. Once we were on our
way, I turned them back on at their lowest setting. She allowed me
to check her vital signs, which were within a range that caused me
not to be concerned. My job now was to keep her calm, monitor
her, and respect her privacy. I called the hospital on my cell phone
because I did not want to do it by radio and have anyone with a
scanner be able to hear what I had to report to the nurse in charge.
The hospital was great. When we arrived, they had a full specially
trained staff waiting, and a female minister. She was in the best
hands available. This was mid-way through my evening shift, and I
was on a double shift that evening and was there until the morning.
Each time I brought a patient to that hospital, I took a moment to
stop in a see her. I was only with her for just under an hour. It is
amazing how attached you become to a patient in a short period. A
few weeks later, I saw the police officer that was so helpful at the
crime scene. I asked her whatever came out of that case.

The outcome was very saddening, but I understood. It was
not the first time I had seen this happen. The young girl was in
counseling. The parents had talked her into not pressing charges,
and she did not identify those that did this to her. Their house was
for sale, and they were moving. Being a parent, although I may
have done something different, I can understand why the parents
would want to move on. No one would look at his or her daughter
the same way. Ridiculous rumors and cruel things would probably
be sad. This would make the news. She would be in the public eye.
It was very sad she had to experience this, and those that did this to
her got away with it, possibly to do it again.

Rape is a violent and brutal crime. However, only one form of
sexual abuse. There are others not as violent. There is no way of
knowing how many of these types of sexual crimes go unreported.
I would guess that number is staggering. Anyone who goes
through this must be prepared to face his or her assailants in open
court and relive the moment, and experience a horrific degree of
embarrassment as attorneys try to discredit them. I wrote his or her

although men do not face violent and brutal rape at the hands of women. At least I could not find any documented cases of it. In the business world, there are cases of a female boss doing something that causes a male subordinate to have slept with them unwillingly, not forcefully. Although not rape in the sense of this 19-year-old girl, it is a form of sexual abuse. There are other forms of sexual abuse as well that may not be physical at all. It could be repeated flirting after being asked many times to stop. It could be in the form of sexual innuendoes, or in the form of what clothes someone wears to direct their attention to a specific individual. It could also be simple touching. Such as rubbing a hand across a person's leg, or putting it on his or her knee, putting your arm around someone, or offering a harmless kiss on the cheek. People refer to their "Personal Space." Being overly close to someone or touching him or her violates that space. Here is where it becomes difficult, and sometimes may not be mal-intended. Oh, did that raise an eyebrow? Relax. It gets back to my original statement about defining terms. Everyone perceives these little things differently. Sometimes, this can cause a problem. Let me give you an example. Younger people tend to be more physical with their friends. Meaning, when they greet one another, they may exchange a kiss on the cheek, a hug, or both. To them, this is normal behavior. Therefore, this is how they react. Place them in a situation where this behavior does not occur, and you have a problem. It is innocent in their eyes, but maybe not to the other person. This was their learned behavior.

I grew up in a 100% Italian household. When I was growing up, this was acceptable behavior. It showed a sign of respect or showing someone you care about them as a person. Put that out in the world today, and it creates a social problem, one that can lead down the wrong path. What one person views as innocent, another may not. In today's society, the only way to avoid that is to be consistent. If not, an error in judgment can always occur. The human condition dictates that people will act according to their learned behaviors. Now, when they act that way, which to them is normal and acceptable, it offends someone. That person may report it. By law, in most states, everyone who works has to take some type of sexual harassment course given by their employer. A study done by *theatlantic.com/education* institute determined that approximately more than 40 percent of students cheat on online courses. What does that mean?

If I or anyone else, take a mandatory online course, passes it and write down the correct answers, they can share them with their co-workers. That is more realistic then everyone being honest. We all know what happens at every job, even in schools. Workers now click through the slides, never take the course, get to the exam, and pass it. Everyone is happy. The company met the legal requirements, and the co-workers did not have to spend hours doing it. All is right in the world. However, is it? Of course not, because over 40% of the people did not learn a thing. This is also a problem at the college level with their regular courses. The point being, there are other forms of sexual abuse or harassment, and their definitions are only governed by how that particular person perceives it. I know a person that was terminated by someone who overheard a conversation and was offended by it. My first question is; if you are not part of the conversation, why are you even listening, let alone reporting someone for what was said. Do you always look around to see who might hear what you are saying? Sometimes, it is innocent.

I ask you this, in some instances, are we going too far. If two men or two women are having a conversation and they are not aware that someone is listening, should they be held responsible? Some may say yes, others no. Has society gotten to the point that to have a conversation somewhere, each person has to wear a device like in the TV series, *"Get Smart?"* For those of you that remember it, it was called "The Cone of Silence."

We live in a world where types of accounts can be hacked. Even our government agencies with the best firewalls and encryption software available have been hacked. Viruses and other things are embedded into emails that get into your computer or cell phone. With millions of people subscribing to VPN services, there is no way to trace where they came from. How many of your friends have sent you a Social Media friend request because their accounts were hacked? It happens. How do we decide what is accidental or intentional? This leaves one important question. Where is the line drawn? There are also people in the world that will bait someone. What does that mean?

That means they will talk with people about anything, seven days a week. Now everyone is comfortable talking about anything until one day that person has a bad day. Something is said that is normally said, and that person becomes offended. This has happened to scores of people. You may have had this experience with a close friend. You try to explain it, but at the time, it makes no difference. Is there an answer? Can people actually walk around each day thinking out each word before they say it? Can people look at every piece of data on their computer before they use it? Isn't that why we buy software, to do that for us? That works on what is known. However, before something is known, it has to happen. So yes, like it or not, the possibility of accidental things happening is strong and alive. As a writer, I have to watch every word I write so as not to offend people. This is more predominant when referring to topics that involve race, color, or creed, as well as sexual preferences. Even in a marriage or partnership, how many times have you joked with your partner about something and it is laughed off? Then one day, it becomes a problem. We live in a highly sensitive society. Do people have the broad shoulders that did years ago?

On the other hand, was society years ago different? Maybe the openness on the silver screen, television, or other media platforms caused people to loosen up, be more open with their thoughts, or become more sensitive. This issue is a result of many sources, not just one. As you can see, the abuse topic is very wide, and not all things fit into a simple definition. The simpler things apply to both men and women. However, men are tolerable and less apt to report something versus women. As much as society has evolved when it comes to gender equality, it is still far from perfect and equal. Some woman still feels vulnerable when dealing with a man, whereas many men still feel superior to women. We have quite a few years to go before that playing field will be equal. For this reason, women are much more cautious than men are. Especially on dating sites. Look up the data. A man will give out his phone number on the first email exchange, yet, a woman will not. She needs some reassurance first. There is always the exception to the rules, but we are speaking in general. Trust me. I have female friends that are quite proficient in the martial arts. I would rather fight a man than one of them, and even they are careful. Let us move on.

Abuse is seen everywhere. Over the past few years, women, and rightfully so, have become much more open about the abuse they feel they have suffered. They are now bringing up things that are years, or decades old. Primarily because when it occurred, no one would listen. Today, more people are listening. The "GOOD OLE BOY" club is not as strong as it was years ago as it relates to some forms of female abuse.

To summarize this chapter, abuse is anything or any action that someone performs that offends another, PERIOD! Nothing makes deliberate abuse right. Some types of abuse are clear-cut, and others can sit in a grey area. In the workplace, the major issues are more about discrimination. Therefore, society can be quite trying at times. What is acceptable today, may not be tomorrow, and changes the following day. This problem will always exist when there is human interaction. Many determining factors affect the way people respond on a day-to-day basis, and social circles vary. This is why consistency is key. Words such as "Accidental" would have never been conceived there was never something that was accidental. The word "Unknown" would have never been conceived if we had all the answers.

CHAPTER 2

TYPES OF ABUSE

Now that we have covered some of the basics, it is time to get into the meat of what this book is all about; *A Woman's Fear.* Some might say, what does a woman have to fear? The courts always rule in their favor. That is the farthest thing from the truth. Most states are now no-fault states in the case of divorce, and some even do divorces online. Talk about enabling the *"Everything is disposable"* concept. The latest data I could find was from *www. census.gov* from 2013. It was estimated that 13.4 million parents lived with 22.1 million children under 21 years of age while the other parent(s) lived somewhere else. 17.5% of those parents that had custody of the children were men. That means 82.5% of parents that have custody of the children were female. Without going any further, that should tell you what a woman has to fear. There is data on deadbeat dads.

However, most studies agree that the data is more of a guideline and may not be very accurate because the laws in some states vary. Many times child support payments come in the form of school tuitions, clothing, or other things that have been agreed upon. Therefore, they are not paid to the ex-spouse on a weekly basis. However, the rule of thumb according to a Time magazine report stated that 66 out of 95 dads were full deadbeat dads. Meaning, they contributed nothing. I do not want to spend a great deal of time on statistics, the point is, in many cases, the woman has something to fear, income. This brings us to the most common type of abuse, domestic abuse. It is the most common because it involves the greatest amount of different forms of abuse. Unlike a workplace, where there may be sexual harassment of some form, domestic violence has managed to take in every aspect of abuse.

- Physical Abuse
- Mental Abuse
- Emotional Abuse
- Verbal Abuse
- Rape

Rape you say, how can a husband rape his wife? Remember, rape is a brutal, criminal, and violent sexual crime. If a husband comes home intoxicated, his wife chooses not to perform, and he hits her and forces himself on her against her will, he has raped her. There is nothing in the definition of rape that does not apply because of a wedding ring and marriage license. Do not think that does not happen. The biggest finding of this type of event it that it is almost never a stand-alone event. When a complete history of the relationship is studied, it is usually found there were many warning signs or smaller events that have been happening that led to this that had gone unaddressed. Why is that? Because that is part of the woman's fear. Let me tell you another true story. I used to respond to a house on many occasions, and I am sure when I was not working, other ambulance may have gone there as well. It was always for a domestic violence call. Many times, it was a push or a shove, an argument that got out of hand, or a slap to the face. A neighbor would call 9-1-1. Not every time did the wife have to go to the hospital, but there were times she did. When she did not go, it was a police matter, and we left. From what I understood, she never would press charges against her husband. One time I was dispatched there. When I arrived, you could see the welts from current slaps, and the healing bruises from previous hits. Her chief complaint was arm pain. She also has a cut on the corner of her lip that would need stitches. This time, it was not an option. She had to go to the hospital. During the exam, we always find out the events that led to the injuries. She claimed she fell. With the history of calls to this address, and old bruises, as well as the new ones, it was my opinion she did not fall. I reported this to the officer at the scene.

As I was splinting her arms and bandaging her lip, the officer interviewed her. By the questions he was asking, I knew he was thinking the same thing. Her husband had a history of excessive drinking and had one DUI on his record from a few years back. He denied hitting her, and she denied him hitting her. After the officer took her statement, we started for the hospital. She thanked me for caring for her. I stated, "(unnamed), I have been doing this job for many years. These injuries are not a result of a fall. However, that is not for me to judge. I do have to give the hospital my findings." She begged me not to suggest her husband hit her. She explained she had three children, all under high school age. She could only work part-time which was not enough to support the kids. She had no family and had nowhere she could go. She could never support keeping the house. Even if she got divorced, her husband would drink the money he made away.

This woman felt stuck there until the children were old enough. I explained to her there were systems in place to assist her, and the hospital staff could help her. The police would see to it that he would not be able to come near her. She would not have it and was getting very upset. I did not talk about it any further. Being a mandated reporter, I was obligated to report this to the officer that was following us to the hospital, as well as the hospital staff, which I did. As it turned out, a complete investigation was performed; the department of children and families was involved. The children were temporarily removed from the home and were allowed to stay with the grandparents of the father. Instead of being arrested, he had to enter a program and counseling. I found out months later he did. We had not been called to the house for some time. We tend to remember the calls we go to a lot. I assumed that all was going well, and never gave it another thought. I remember this so clearly. It was a Saturday night. I was called to see if I could do an overnight shift. I could use the overtime and had nothing planned, so I took the shift.

It was about two-thirty in the morning. I remember the time because we had just brought a patient back to a skilled nursing facility from the hospital in that same town. I remember looking at my watch and telling my partner, "I'm starving. I'm going to call dispatch to find out if we could stop at the all-night diner to get something to go." When I was on the phone with dispatch, they gave me the okay to get a bite to eat then suddenly said, "Hold on." When they got back on the phone, they said, "Sorry, maybe later, I need you to respond to (xxxxxxx) for an unresponsive female. Yes. You guessed it. It was that address. We were only six blocks away from the call and got there before the police and fire department. We ran in with our gear, the police arrived seconds later. There she was on the bed. She presented with numerous healing bruises, and there were three open and empty pill bottles on the bed. She was not breathing, and I could not feel a pulse. As we were tending to her, the fire department arrived. While we were performing our initial care, they got us a backboard so we could carry her out to our stretcher. My partner was doing CPR while I established other treatment methods along with the paramedic from the fire department. We had a great deal of help on the scene. The fire department did an excellent job of speeding the transfer process of getting her from her room, and into our ambulance. The paramedic and I worked hard to get her back. About four blocks from the hospital, we got a pulse back and good heart rhythm. By the time we brought her into the emergency room, she was starting to breathe on her own. Everything after that was taken care of by the police and the hospital. She survived. Most times, we do not know the intimate details of the outcome of these cases.

In this case, about two months later, we were taking a woman back to a shelter for battered women. She was fine and walked in. After the staff signed our paperwork, I felt a tap on my shoulder. I turned, and there she was. She looked great. Like a new person. She was leaving that week. Her husband was arrested, she was getting a divorce, and the kids had been staying with their grandparents and would be returning home the following week. The program she was in helped her and would continue to assist her. She planned on selling the house and getting a smaller one that she could afford. She gave me a huge hug and thanked me. I told her the best thanks she gave me was seeing her here that day and knowing she was on the right track. This case had a happy conclusion, but not until after a near-death experience. As it turned out, her husband was drunk that night, and one of the children got up to go to the bathroom because they did not feel well. When the child walked in her room, the child could not wake up either parent. Luckily, the child dialed 9-1-1. Another ten minutes and there would have been no getting her back. Not every person is that lucky.

Getting over the physical injuries from rape goes much quicker than getting over the emotional ones. There was a woman in one group I spoke with that was raped. She was a married woman. It took almost a year before she was able to be intimate with her husband again. There are also cases where this has led to divorce. It takes a great deal of time and understand, and yes, counseling, to get through this. The emotional effects can go well beyond that of just the victims. Although the victims carry the most weight, all aspects must be considered to move forward. In a relationship, what affects one person also affects the other, as well as their family and friends.

Many times domestic violence begins with verbal abuse, name-calling, and yelling. It can turn into a push or shove, eventually a slap, and escalate. Not all domestic violence cases end up this way. My point is, it needs to be addressed when it starts, so it does not escalate. I stated earlier, in almost every case of more serious domestic violence cases, there were warning signs. Even with this, I want to make this perfectly clear. There is no excuse for any man to do this. Even in the case of infidelity, walk away and move on. Deal with it legally. DO NOT confuse this with someone who is attacking you and you need to defend yourself. That is a completely different subject and not for this book.

Mental and Emotional abuse is what I call the slow killer. It builds up over the years. It could range from a variety of things, or a combination of things. We live in a society now where the vast majority of marriages are two income families. Meaning, both the husband and the wife works. The major complaint from married women is the husband does not help. Many times they are referring to cleaning, cooking, laundry, the children, is irrelevant. Over time, that falls under the heading of emotional abuse, especially when the wife has been bringing this to her husband's attention for some time, and he has done nothing to correct that behavior. She will get frustrated, angry, feel used, which all can lead to some form of depression. Depression can lead to other medical problems. It affects a person's self-worth, self-esteem, and they feel trapped, especially when children are involved. In many cases, the mother is the primary nurturing figure.

Another form of mental and emotional abuse can occur when a husband constantly takes his wife for granted. He never displays any signs of appreciation but wants all the benefits that go along with a marriage. He wants a house cleaner, a cook, a mother, and a sex toy. All while she is also working. In its own way, this type of abuse is just as damaging. We also must keep in mind that every woman is different and will react differently to the same issue.

Another form and maybe the worst form of mental and emotional abuse is the flirt. The man who goes out to dinner, or anywhere with his partner and flirts with every woman, and watches every woman that walks into a room, often times even commenting on her or directly comparing her to his partner. This is demeaning behavior. It would make any woman feel inferior and hurt. Eventually, that woman will not want to go anywhere with that man. If she does, it is because he has now created mistrust between them. She may be thinking, if he does this in my presence, what does he do if I am not there?

I stated on in the introduction at times, I speak at women support groups. I do this because of my real world experience in the medical field, and yes, some personal experiences. I feel there is much I can offer to these women because of my training and experience. I never charge a fee to do this. Here is a story from a nice woman I met when I spoke to a group. It directly relates to my last thoughts. She had been married for almost twenty years before she divorced her husband. She stated he never hit her, called her names, or anything of that nature. He was an executive. He was required to attend many events. These events were the type of events where he needed to have his wife with him as his escort since everyone else would. His problem was, no matter where they went, even if it was to a store, he always looked at other women. Sometimes saying he was going to a different department in the store. She would notice when he walked away, he was heading in the direction of a woman he was looking at. As she put it, "If we went to dinner, he would scope out every bitch in the room, or anyone who walked in." Over the years, she explained he would always make comments to her about a woman he saw. "What a nice ass she had, or her hair color."

He would make statements such as, "Why can't you be a little taller like her." She also mentioned other things such as clothing, and other body parts. She explained she raised this issue to him so many times, and all he would say is, "You're too sensitive." She

15

went on to say that at first if he commented on the hair color of another woman, she would dye her hair. He would ask why she did that. When she explained, he would tell her she was ridiculous. In time, she stopped. She felt there was no making him happy. She went to counseling, and he refused to go. She said she felt there was no point of going alone, so she stopped going. Over time, she stopped going anywhere with him and did not care what he did. She felt she was not good enough for him, and something was wrong with her. At one point, she started to flirt with other men just to get some attention. Slowly she was becoming more depressed. She had no self-esteem or self-worth. One day she made what to her was an innocent comment to a girlfriend. Her friend was telling her to leave him for some time. She always thought he was probably cheating on her. She explained, "Some days I wish I were dead." She never attempted to harm herself, and we all know that many people say such things with no intention of doing it. Her friend called 9-1-1 because she was worried about her. As it turned out, she went to the hospital, it was straightened out, and she was released.

She went on to say she went back to counseling which she said was a great help. As she began to feel good about herself again, she filed for divorce. After a couple of years, she met someone who treated her the way she wanted to be treated and appreciated her. She was now coming to these sessions to help others. As she put it, "It was a great reminder for her to never tolerate that type of abuse again." Everyone has a story to tell. I was amazed at how open these women were to talk amongst themselves about their experiences. I think they accepted me because of some of the stories I told them through my experiences as a paramedic, and I was a good listener if they asked. I think this degree of honesty is what made them realize I was sincere in wanting to help.

Verbal Abuse. You will see me write many times that any form of abuse is unacceptable. However, each has their own inherent traits. To the person experiencing it at the time, it is the worst type of abuse because it is directly affecting them. Verbal abuse is not a one and done. It continues, and at times, relentlessly. In a counseling session I spoke at, I heard a woman's story. She was in her late thirties and had two children. I would classify her as having an about average build. I assume from her story, at one time she was slender. I am guessing that her body type changes after having two children. Her story was that she was having a difficult time because her husband constantly embarrassed her, at home, and in public. She explained that one night; they were out to dinner with friends. We all know that every restaurant brings out bread. She mentioned she was trying to get back down to her size 6 dress. She was now a size 10.

She was always able to lose weight easily before she had her children, but now, even with exercising 4 times a week, it was a challenge. This is a common story for many women. She only ordered a salad. When she reached for a small, and she emphasized a small piece of bread, her husband made a comment, "Bread? Do you really think you need that? She said she wanted to break down and cry. She added that he always made these types of comments. She stated even when they shared intimate moments together; he would make a comment about her waistline and other personal things. He once made this comment, "Your breasts aren't firm anymore." She finally had reached a point where she was depressed and had no self-esteem. This was why she joined this group. Imagine living with these types of comments day after day. Regardless of where you are, or the company you are in. This is a constant form of torture. Do people end relationships because of this? Yes, they do. However, in general, women are more emotional than men are. They will stick it out until the very end and try to fix it.

I once responded to a sick call. As it turned out, the woman was suffering from bulimia. Bulimia is a serious and potentially life-threatening eating disorder. After eating, people will purge themselves, meaning, force themselves to vomit to get rid of the extra calories. This is a very unhealthy way to do this. When we arrived, I noticed an obvious undernourished woman. Her husband stated she eats every day. This automatically raised a red flag for me. She was in her mid-forties. Her husband stated her weight loss only began over the past five or six months and had no medical history or problems. Her last physical was seven months ago and went well. No problems were noted. Could she have developed a fast developing cancer? Of course, that could be a possibility. However, she did not present with the other markers I would have expected to see. I knew there was more to this story. She was dehydrated, which was also apparent by looking at her and checking her vital signs. As it turned out, she would not eat all day. At dinner, she would be so hungry she would overeat. Go into the bathroom, and force herself to throw up. Currently, the exact cause of this condition is unknown. However, it is believed that multiple factors contribute to this disorder. They can be genetic, psychological, stress, and more. It is the job of the clinician to try to find out the underlying cause.

Later in my shift, I saw she was going to be admitted. I went over to see here. She thanked me and said, "I don't want you to think I am a nut case. I do this so I can keep my weight down because my husband always was telling me I was getting fat." BINGO! There is it. I asked her if she had told this to her nurse and doctor. She said she had. They were admitting her because some of her blood work was off and they wanted to correct it. Hippa laws are very strict. A clinician cannot discuss a case with anyone who is not part of that case. I was able to ask the physiatrist what she thought because I was the paramedic that brought her in. This was a classic case of stress secondary to social complications. Her husband would be spoken to, and I am sure they would have to do some counseling. I hope that it would have a positive outcome.

There are many forms of verbal abuse. Some include insults, comments during intimate moments, constant complaining about someone to that person, embarrassment, and more. In time, if not corrected, they can lead to many problems, and be the cause of infidelity, and in some cases suicide attempts. It leads to severe forms of depression. If could early, these things can be fixed. If not, it can lead to life-long medications and therapy. It can lead to drug use and abuse. It can destroy a person's life. In that same session, there was a woman there because after getting out of a relationship that involved domestic violence, she could not have a successful relationship, or at times, even start one, regardless of how interested she was in the person. She could not get over the fear of what she went through. There was another woman there that also had the same issue. It was a great group discussion. I found it quite interesting when she asked me a question.

Her question was, "As a man, how would you handle a situation if you dated someone with that past." I must say that first I had to state that every man is different, and have different levels of understanding. I asked one question of both women. I asked, "When you met anyone that wanted to date you, did you tell them of your history." Both women replied no. I asked why. Although their answers were slightly different, the meaning was the same. They did not feel that was the time to tell anyone something that personal. I agreed and asked, "If you dated them for some time, did you tell them? They both replied no.

I asked them to look at it from a different perspective. I explained, there was no need for them to go into details, however, to think about it this way. Is it fair to another if you do not let them know of the issue? How could you expect them to understand? In their eyes, they may perceive it as you not being interested and walk away because you have been holding. We need to give people the opportunity to decide if they could go slow and give you the time. Just think about how that would reduce the stress. Before I continue with the story, let me add a couple of things to the mix.

1. Not every man is the same,
2. You can't judge every man based upon your past experience,
3. If you are expecting someone to give you a chance, should you do the same?

Past bad experiences are some of the most difficult things to get over. They leave scars, and sometimes, permanent ones. That does not mean a person cannot move on. Let us get back to the story. I explained that I dated a girl once who told me immediately that she had a bad emotional experience in her past relationship. She really enjoyed my company, but she wanted me to know it would take her time to be herself. Maybe because of my medical background I was able to be more understanding than most. Other men may also be that understanding, and others may not want the baggage. We all have baggage. I explained to them we dated for some time and things took their natural course. We only stopped seeing each other because our long-term goals were different. However, we made it past her past. What was amazing was that they never thought of doing that. I explained that pressure, stress, and/or fear, hold us back every time. I explained that you could be letting someone walk out of your life that should be there. I also added, "With that said, once you present your situation to a man, and he chooses to walk away, that is not the man you should be with anyway." We continued with a very good exchange of thoughts and ideas. These are some of a woman's fears. The things she thinks about and has to live with.

Let us look at another situation. One that many forget exists. Some women have been abused at a young age by a parent or relative. These leave very deep scars. Their self-respect and self-esteem have been torn from them before they were old enough to understand it. When they do, it hits them like a ton of bricks. The feelings, emotions, and memories of the events, come rushing with the intensity of water from a broken dam. This is intensified further when it was a situation where they never told anyone. They kept it buried inside. Anything we bury inside can one day resurface. Something will happen to trigger it and bring it to the surface. At the time, they had no support system, or anyone to turn to. I have been to many calls for depression or attempted suicides for young women because they have no self-worth, and have abused their bodies so badly that they just want it to end. They may have reached an age when they understand what has happened, and it comes rushing to the surface. Many times these emotions may not surface for years. As I stated, as people, we bury things deep inside. It could take years for them to surface.

A call I vividly remember was for a woman in her late twenties. She had only been married for two years, and her marriage was fine. One night while in bed with her husband, they were started to become intimate. According to her husband, he stated, "Out of nowhere, she just snapped, she went nuts, and curled up in the corner of the room and would not let me come near her."

That night I was working with a female partner who started to talk to the young woman. Her condition was emotional and not life-threatening at this time. I let my partner talk to her. As I interviewed the husband, he stated, "She has never done anything like this before." I needed to ask if the intimate part of their relationship was normal. He replied, "It was great." She made no advances to try to harm herself, or be violent towards us in any way.

She just was curled up with a blanket around her trembling in the corner. Not knowing the full story, I asked the husband to wait outside of the room. The police wanted to speak with him as well. A firefighter, my partner, and I were the only people in the room with the woman. After some time, my partner managed to help her get dressed while we waited by the door. My partner did an excellent job of talking with her and calming her down. We brought her to the hospital. We later found out that she was a victim of child sexual abuse. The doctor said maybe the husband said one word or made a certain advance that triggered that memory. Often times it only takes the smallest thing to trigger a memory. In this case, it was a bad memory. Many times, they can manifest years later.

A paramedic is specially trained in many areas. They are the first line of defense. Their job, although many think it is just to give someone a ride to the hospital, is to save lives. Not every call is life and death, but at times, to a patient, what they are experiencing is similar to life to death to them. A paramedic must have training, compassion, be a good listener, have excellent people skills, and be able to function under the worst of situations and conditions. Anyone that ever said to me, "Oh, you're an ambulance driver;" I would reply, "Really, is that what you think? Spend a day with me in the back of a rig and tell me if that is what I am." You never see people smile. You never see them during their good times. You interact with them and their families when something has gone wrong. Being a Paramedic can be emotionally and physically draining; a job that also suffers from a high suicide rate. In a survey done in 2017 by *firerescue1.com*, of the 4000 first responders surveyed, 6.6% stated they have attempted to commit suicide. That is ten times the rate of the public. In an article by the New York Daily News on April 12[th,] 2018, *http://www.nydailynews. com/news/national/responders-die-suicide-job-article-1.3930162,* they stated in 2017, 103 firefighters and 140 police officers took their own lives, as compared to 93 firefighters and 129 police officers who died in the line of duty. Add that to the 6.6% that attempted to take their own life, and you have some gravely alarming numbers. The job takes its toll. After 30+ years of it, I knew it was my time to end that career. However, I learned so much about people and life.

Besides all the blood and guts, you see it all. You will see people like you are I whose bodies have been torn apart in a car accident, those who have shot most of their head off with a shotgun, and so much more. However, you also get to help those that need it. Deliver a few babies and bring new life into the world. It is all about the balance. For me, especially when it comes to the topic of female abuse, it always bothered me that I never would see how someone survived that trauma. How they were doing after getting help. This is why I am so passionate about speaking at these women's support groups. It is my way of knowing many survived and are working through it.

Let us turn to education for a moment. Over the past couple of years, this has been more prevalent in the news. Not because someone is inventing a new wheel, this has been going on for years. Now, people are more comfortable speaking out and reporting it. Some teachers have had an affair with their student; a coach that abused those on the team; a college professor who in the sanctuary of his office uses that as a platform to meet with a student and make sexual comments or advances. All it takes is one individual that has the strength and courage to speak out and bring it out in the open. Once that person does, others step up. We have all seen that on the news. One day it is one person that makes the news. In a few days, others step up and admit they were victims. Why does this all take so much time? That will be discussed in another chapter. This form of abuse has been steadily on the rise. We can only hope that with the media coverage this receives, that stops those that initiate this form of abuse stop for fear of being exposed. However, in many cases, it is a sickness. Often times, one they cannot control. That is why I always tell women that "FEAR" is never the answer. Fear only breeds more fear. Eventually, fear becomes a trap. A trap that becomes almost impossible to escape without help. The first step in solving any problem is realizing there is one.

CHAPTER 3

OTHER FORMS OF ABUSE, OR NOT?

This is the controversial chapter. The chapter where many may agree, and others disagree. First, let me state that this book is not written based on my opinions. However, before I move forward, we must agree to be open-minded and realize that whether we like something or not, whether we agree with it or not. The truth is ALWAYS the truth. We may not like it, but we must be able to accept it. There are many organizations to help women. The one I support is the "METOO" movement. With all the laws, with all the movements, and with all the resources, things will still happen. All we can do to be there to help people. However, we cannot close our eyes to some realities. There is a big difference between abuse and exploitation. With that established, women that knowingly, for financial gain, or willing under their own free will consent to something, IS NOT ABUSE. Providing, there is no form of abuse during the process. We all have choices. There have been many times in my life I could have looked away from my own values and morals for advancement. It was my choice not to. However, if I had chosen to, that would be my choice. No one put a gun to my head to make that choice. Let us not confuse abuse, what with someone does based on their free will. Let us look at the definition of free will, courtesy of Merriam-Webster. The definition of free will has two parts.

1: voluntary choice or decision - I do this of my own *free will*
2: freedom of humans to make choices that are not determined by prior causes or by divine intervention

Let us be clear. This portion only applies if there is no form of abuse associated with it.

Therefore, someone who has exchanged sexual favors for advancement is NOT abuse in the manner that the word abuse is used. If certainly is **unethical** for someone to make those types of offers, but it is not abuse. The party involved had the option NOT to accept. Now that you are ready to shoot me, that is the truth from a literal fact.

From a moral fact, it stinks. No one should put a woman in that position. In a perfect world, whoever is best qualified for any position should be the one to receive it, regardless of race, color, creed, or gender. When that principle is not followed, it is discrimination. Is discrimination a form of abuse? Yes, because it can lead to emotional abuse. Let me give you another example. If a porn star chooses to pose with no clothes on to advertise their film, some may see that as exploitation. However, they are doing it willingly and being paid for it. The same applies to suggestive scenes in a movie. In these cases, people use the term *"Art form."*

Yes, some may not like it, and many women may feel offended by it and see it as a way of exploiting women. There are also women that will take the stand that it is that person's right to express themselves as they choose. In these cases, there is no true right or wrong. It is a matter of opinion. Another point I must address is that **at times,** someone will make these things public years later for financial gain. Again, you do not have to like that, but it is a reality. There are also cases when this was attempted where the actual findings proved otherwise. Although in the grand scheme of things, these cases are not the norm, however, they do exist. The world does have what is called, "Opportunists" in it.

Where the problem comes in this situation is in a class action suit. Many will join the cause. All it takes is for one person to prove an accusation, and everyone wins. That is why it is a class action suit. The others may only have to prove opportunity, meaning, they had contact with that person. Many acknowledge this as being a reality, and some will not even entertain the fact that this is true. We must remain objective to separate the problem and institute the solutions.

Unethical business practices have been going on for years. No one invented the wheel here. However, some of these practices place a woman in a very difficult position for a variety of reason.

- They need to keep their job
- They need to advance to make more money
- They have specific career goals
- Possibly due to their past, they have self-esteem issues
- The saddest reason being, it has been an accepted practice

These tie in with other issues. Remember, this entire subject is a tangled web, and many things intertwine with others. For years, studies have shown that the main reason for infidelity in males is due to their exposure to opportunity. It could be traveling a lot for business, exposure at the workplace, and the fact that many men would go out while their partners were at home. The studies have not changed. These are easily researched on the internet. Now, infidelity by women has increased for the same reasons since women now have advanced in the equality setting. Therefore, their exposure and risk factors have increased. Much of this is not by choice. The human condition tells us that by nature, any two people that do not spend time together will get their needs filled elsewhere. A woman I spoke with at one meeting was telling me her story. It represented that exact theory. She was divorced, but still loved her husband. He traveled a lot because of his job. He was a production engineer and had to travel to different manufacturing plants, some being overseas. She never thought he was unfaithful to her. Her kids were older, and only one was still living home and in the last year of college. She worked in advertising and received a promotion. This promotion required her to travel occasionally to one of the other business offices. She would work with the manager of that office. They reached a point that they spend much less time together, and when they were home together, they were often tired. A psychology profession I had once said in a lecture, "Given the right set of circumstances, anyone is capable of infidelity." Let's look at some data from 2017 courtesy of *https://www.trustify.info/blog/infidelity-statistics-2017.*

Infidelity Statistics

- In over 1/3 of marriages, one or both partners admit to cheating.
- 22% of men say that they have cheated on their significant other.
- 14% of women admit to cheating on their significant other.
- 36% of men and women admit to having an affair with a coworker.
- 17% of men and women admit to having an affair with a sister-in-law or brother-in-law.
- People who have cheated before are 350% more likely to cheat again.
- Affairs are most likely to occur two years into a marriage.
- **35% of men and women admit to cheating while on a business trip.**
- 9% of men admit they might have an affair to get back at a spouse.
- 14% of women admit they might have an affair to get back at a spouse.
- 10% of affairs begin online.
- 40% of the time online affairs turn into real life affairs.

She went on to tell me that on one of her trips, she and the manager went out for dinner at the end of the workday. She freely admitted she drank too much and the unthinkable happened. She did something she had never done or thought she ever would. She was unfaithful. She further explained that this bothered her to the point that when she returned, she quit her job. She was very emotional disturbed by this and felt she needed to be honest with her husband who was due to return from his trip in two days. When he returned, she was completely honest and told him what happened and why. She also told him she quit her job. She was sorry and wanted to work this out. She felt that no job they would have or the money they could make was worth losing their marriage. She explained that she had reached a point that she was lonely, and felt alone all the time. Her husband could not accept this and file for divorce. She did not try to stop it. She felt it was her fault. She was going to these meetings to get help in coping with this. Ask yourself these questions:

1. Is she the only one at fault?
2. Could this have been avoided?
3. Where and when did the breakdown of this relationship begin?

Those are just a few of the questions, and come up with your answers. I will not comment on them because the purpose of this exercise is to make you think, and once again, it is a matter of beliefs and opinions. You may be wondering, what does this have to do with the topic of this book? Keep in mind, that not all abuse is physical. Actually, as I stated earlier, the majority of abuse is emotional, and at different levels. When we look at abuse as a subject, we must consider all forms of abuse. Remember, to this woman, this was as devastating in her mind to her, as someone who was hit by a spouse. This reason for this is, in the human mind, what affects us personally, is viewed as the most devastating event. Very few compare what is going on with them to what is going on with others that in reality is far worse. That is simply the human rational.

Before we move on, let us look at some other data. According to the National Voice of Domestic Violence, a woman will leave an abusive relationship seven times before she leaves for good. While we are on this subject, here is the phone number for the national domestic abuse hotline. It is available 24/7. (800) 799-SAFE (7233).

"A Woman's Fear." Why seven times? There are many reasons.

1. They feel it is dangerous. Maybe a threat has been made.
2. Children

3. Finances or no support system
4. The ever made promise that it will never happen again
5. Love
6. Fear of being alone
7. Low self-esteem
8. Maybe they feel some of it is their fault because the other person blames them for their behavior
9. Fear of what others may think
10. They hope things will change

The list goes on. This type of situational abuse encompasses many forms of abuse all at the same time. Once any woman reaches a point of hopelessness, they feel defeated. They can no longer fight back. They succumb to their situation and try to make the best of it.

It was my job as a paramedic to be objective, and not subjective. That is easier said than done. When you respond to a call involving a case when a child has been abused, you fight every emotion you have not to do or say something stupid. Often times the parents are so protective they will not allow the child to be examined for fear of what you will find out. You have to keep your head. It is a game of wits. The care and the safety of any child ALWAYS come first. Most parents are normally protective of their children, as a health care provider you must be able to determine whether that is a normal response, or there are underlying reasons. We are also specially trained to be able to determine the difference, remembering that every case is different, and people react differently to a given situation. If you lose your focus and allow your emotions to rule your judgment, the outcome can be devastating. Many might be wondering why I mentioned the suicide rates amongst first responders earlier. Being a first responder is one of the most stressful jobs anyone can do. As a firefighter, I have had to rescue a victim that was still alive in a burning car, only to grab them and have the skin of their arm slip off them in between the fingers of my gloves. Deal with that emotion and visual picture while you now have to try to save their life.

The reason for this last paragraph was to lead into this next story. This is a story of female abuse but in a different form. It was emotional abuse, but she was not the only victim. This story will show how other circumstances can affect how a person reacts. I think all would agree that a mother is nurturing, and will protect their child at all costs. When the circumstances dictate otherwise, that statement may not always be true. My role as a speaker at the meeting I attended was more to answer questions. To help them understand the underlying reasons or causes, and realize they are not alone. I do not want to use the word enjoy, because that gives the wrong perception, let me say they listen intently as I would tell a story about a call I had during my career. They do not need to be lectured or spoken to about abuse. They lived it. At one of this meeting, a woman was having a difficult time telling her story about her child that was abused. One of the things that make these meeting so successful is time. You must give people time to speak when they are ready to. However, there are ways of helping that along. By the bits and pieces she was trying to form, I had the sense of what her situation was. I asked her to take a break and listen to a call I was on.

The call came in as a possible child abuse call. The police were requesting our presence to evaluate a child. When my partner and I arrived, it was clear that the parents were not going to be very helpful. The police had to threaten to arrest them if they did not let me examine the child. Bruises, new or old, can tell a big story. They can give you an idea what caused them by their shape, and the color can tell you how long ago they were sustained. This child had clear-cut signs of being abused. Another sign of child abuse is also when a child will not want to go to one or both parents. I explained to the office on the scene that it was my opinion that this child had been abused. Once that decision is made, the police take custody of the child. They determine if an arrest will be made at that time, or later. The circumstances dictate that decision. All parties involved at some point notify whatever the local agency is that protects children. Here are the circumstances around the female abuse, just in case you lost track of that. In this case, the wife was a substance abuser. Her husband, possibly out of anger, might have been taking his frustrations out on the child. When the mother was coherent enough to know what was going on, she would try to protect her child, which led to the husband threatening her. Out of frustration, she would take her drugs, and the husband could do what he wanted. This is a horrible type of abuse. Not only involves the child, but also the mother. It now involves more than one person. During the investigation on scene, all of this came out. The husband and wife were arrested.

This story must have hit a nerve because the woman at the meeting opened up. As it turned out, I was correct. Her story was very similar, with a minor difference. I do not know the outcome of my case, but this woman explained her child was in foster care, she had to go through a drug rehab program and counseling. After that, she could have minimally supervised visits with her child and had to go for regular drug screenings if she wanted any hope of one day getting her child back, not counting the attorney costs, and hearings she would have to attend. She was attending these meeting to help keep herself focused on the goal of getting her child back. The husband being removed from the equation certainly helped. He was the original cause of her turning to drugs. It was her means of escape. She was quite emotional while she told her story. I was told this only her third meeting. Here was a case of abuse on many levels, and many things failed for it to reach that point. The one thing that always fails is reporting the issue early when help is easiest to obtain, and the worse scenarios could be avoided.

Think back to when I said every person is different. They are, and they will react differently. Therefore, passing judgment on anyone is never the answer. No person can judge another based on how claim they might handle a situation. First, until someone is actually in a situation, they can never be sure what they would do, or how they would react. It is always easy to say, *"If that were me,"* or *"If that happened to me,* "good plan, but not reality. If I had ten cents for every time I heard someone say, *"I never thought I was capable of that,"* I would be rich. Unknown factors and things people have never experienced, people cannot predict what they would do. There is no baseline comparison. It is an unskilled or trained task. However, in the case of a skilled or trained task, your training takes over. You can predict with a degree of accuracy what you would do. This is why firefighters, military personnel, police officers, EMS personnel, and other professions train so much. We can predict our actions. We know our limits, and do not overstep them. Well… most of the time.

Abuse may not always present itself as it seems. This last case was a perfect example. It can involve many levels. At times, people may not even realize there is abuse until it gets out of hand. What have we covered so far? We have covered what abuse is, and the traditional ways it presents itself. We have also covered other types of non-traditional abuse and the many levels it could present itself. Now we need to cover one more. We need to discuss a form of emotional abuse that will shock you, one that most never really consider, but does exist. That is friend or family emotional abuse. "ENVY." What is envy? Envy is a feeling of discontented or resentful longing aroused by someone else's possession, qualities, or luck, or a desire to have those possessions. Some refer to this as "Pathological Jealousy."

Yes, there is a medical condition for this. We cannot choose our family; we can only choose whether we will associate ourselves with them. However, we can choose our friends. *A friend is someone that will not tell you what you want to hear, or tell you something for their own gain. A friend is someone that will tell you the truth.* Well, how does that related to a woman fear? Although the data and research on this are still in its infancy, it is known that men are less likely to give their male friend bad advice. Mostly because men do not talk to each other about personal matters like women do. Therefore, it is assumed that this type of problem is more prevalent in females. There are different stages of emotional growth; therefore, it makes sense that the degree of emotional abuse is also different at various stages of growth. How many times have we told our children when their boyfriend or girlfriend broke up with them in high school? "Don't worry. You will get over it. There are plenty of fish in the sea." Most times, they get over it rather quickly. However, as adults, that hurt is much deeper, probably because of having more bad experiences. The recovery process can take much longer.

I responded to a call for a 15-year-old who was not acting normal and stated she wanted to kill herself. Normal is defined as what is normal for that person. As most know, over the past few years, suicide rates for teens and college-age young adults has skyrocketed. Years ago, that statement was not taken seriously, unless they had a history of a mental disorder. Today, every statement like that is taken seriously. That is a completely separate topic. However, it does have a place in this book. When we arrived, I said with the girl and asked her what was going on. She was very upset. I took a few minutes to calm her down, and she would not talk in front of her parents. I convinced them to leave the room. They could stand outside with the door open, but not be seen. They agreed. As the story goes, she was dating a boy at school. They were having problems, and she was talking to her "best" friend about it. Her best friend eventually talked her into breaking up with him. When she did, her best friend started dating him and stopped talking to her. In the scheme of things, this seems minor compared to the other forms of abuse. However, is it? Could it be the start of what could develop into greater problems later on? Could this be the start of the young girl losing her self-esteem? Keep in mind. Most major problems are a result of smaller ones that went either unnoticed or not addressed. The medical community is constantly learning that much of what happens to us as adults, the choices or decisions we make, are a direct result of our upbringing and experiences. Therefore, the trend now is to clip the wings of these problems when they start, at any age. That starts when people are young. We have covered a great deal in these first three chapters. Now it is time to move on.

CHAPTER 4

AWARENESS

This first step in almost anything in life revolves around awareness. Awareness had many levels. Most have a general awareness of this type of abuse by what they see on the news, read on social media, experience, or the internet. However, this type of awareness is basic, yet a great start. There are different levels of awareness that apply to most things. Dr. Adam Blatner describes them quite well. Here is the link to his article and books. *https://www.blatner.com/adam/psyntbk/fivelevelsawareness.html*

I want to keep this simple and easy to understand since not everyone reading this has medical training. Think of it this way. Our minds are thinking at different levels at the same time. Our conscious mind is thinking about what is going on in the present while our sub-conscious mind is also thinking. The mind uses these two types of consciousness to tie present events to our previous experiences, providing an experience exists that our mind can use as a point of reference. An experience does not mean it has to be something that directly affected you. However, that type of memory will be stronger. It can be an event or something that you were a part of, such as helping a friend. In your mind, this occurs automatically, without conscious thought. Meaning, we do not have to make this happen. Compare it to breathing. You do not consciously have to tell yourself to breathe. It is automatic. Sigmund Freud divided human consciousness into three levels of awareness: conscious, preconscious, and unconscious. Modern psychology has further expanded on that. We are not going that deep into it. These three are enough.

Conscious awareness is the state of quality of awareness or being aware of an external object or something within oneself.

Precocious awareness refers to information that is available for cognitive processing but that currently lies outside conscious awareness.

Unconscious awareness refers more to our dreams and apparent thoughts that appear without any apparent cause. Many theorize that this does not play a significant role in general awareness. I mentioned it only because it is part of the theory.

Those are the basics. You might be asking; how does this apply to this topic? The human mind is an amazing organ. It processes millions of thoughts and tasks simultaneously. However, for our topic of a woman's fear, there needs to be a reference or knowledge point. Without it, these risks increase. As the saying goes, if you do not know about something, you cannot prepare for it.

Awareness starts with education. No one who plans anything that has any degree of risk does it without planning and research. The goal is to make the task as safe as possible by being aware of the risks and taking the correct measures to reduce or eliminate the risk. Research the subject of female abuse. Research the signs a man might display that could make you think this could be a potential problem. We will be discussing that in the next chapter. Situational awareness is very important. It is a tool. The tool you will use to protect yourself. It is the perception of environmental and events concerning time or space, the comprehension of their meaning, and the projection of their future status. Yeah, that can be confusing. Simply put, know what is going on around you. How many times have you been told, or told your daughter, "Never leave your drink unattended." I remember pounding that into my daughters head. At the time of this writing, that is still the number one way "rape date drugs" get into someone's system.

I responded to a call one evening to a house that the parents called because when their daughter came home from a party, she was not acting right. She never drank, and there was no smell of alcohol on her breath. Just by examining her pupils, I knew there was a substance involved other than the possibility of alcohol. The police were on scene and do their investigation. We transported the girl to the emergency room. She was eighteen years ago. As it turns out, something was put in her soda. There was no alcohol in her system. When the boy who took her to the party was picked up by the police, whatever they did in their interrogation resulted in him telling the truth. As it turned out, he did not put the chemical in her soda. He had a friend do it while they were dancing. She was sexually assaulted. This led to two arrests. These things still happen. Although I rarely go out to clubs, I have seen young women dancing with their drinks in their hands, or they will take them to the restroom with them. This is an excellent preventative measure. Although this type of abuse is more prevalent in younger age groups, it speaks to situational awareness.

Awareness is not just about watching what is going on with you, watch what is going on around you. If something does not feel right, most cases it is not. In much of the training I have had, part of it revolved around awareness. A police officer, a firefighter, or medical personnel must constantly be aware of their surroundings. They have to be able to see things developing before they actually do. That is the key to prevention. For a woman, that is not different. If you are out on a date with a newer friend, or even an established one, if you see something developing you do not like, LEAVE! When I was in college, I worked many different part-time jobs. One time I worked as a bouncer. At that age, I will say it was fun work. However, it was also an education; an education in people. Countless times while working as a paramedic I had to deal with extremely violent patients because of their drug or alcohol abuse. Later when you see them restrained in the emergency room and sober, they apologize for their actions. Often times they do not remember the event. A person's baseline personality can change drastically when they are under any form of mind-altering substance. Ask yourself, how many times have you been completely sober and been around intoxicated people? What did you think? I would bet that you could not stand being around them, whether you knew them or not. It is like going out to eat. If you are going to eat something that has a lot of garlic in it, make sure the person you are with is doing the same. You will not smell it on one another's breath. Now, I am NOT advocating you get drunk along with everyone else. It is simply making a point.

Awareness is also drawing upon your experiences. Everyone says, "I don't have baggage and don't take my past into the present, or the future." HOGWASH, everyone has baggage. There is nothing wrong with baggage. It is what you do with it that causes the problem. Baggage or bad experiences are meant to be a learning process. One you take forward. You never blame someone new for what someone else did to you, but you use it as a reference point, so you do not find yourself in that situation again. With that said, many do not learn a thing from their experiences. This is one reason I stated and reference an earlier study that showed women will go back to a bad relationship as many as seven times before they leave it for good. Keep in mind that studies do not mean you will be a statistic. Your actions will determine that. It is a study based on the general population. Situational awareness comes with practice and experience. Like any other task you practice, once you master it, it becomes automatic.

Part of being aware is not running from reality. Women suffer from many forms of abuse. Know them. Do not shy away from listening to someone's story because it is unpleasant. It happens. It is said that experience is the best teacher. In this case, this is something you DO NOT wish to experience. Know what to look for to reduce the risks. We are not talking about the arguments you may get into from time to time with your partner. They are normal. No two people always agree. However, there is a fine line that when crossed, can be the start of a problem. When the arguments become a daily occurrence, there is the potential for a problem. When you cannot communicate your thoughts and fears to your partner, there is a problem. How someone reacts when they are angry is affected by many factors. These factors may change from day-to-day. Stress, money problems, lack of intimacy, children, and others things are just some examples. With that said, this part is a two-way street. I have been to calls where a man has been physically assaulted by a woman. At times, an abusive woman can be the cause of her own abuse. That is primarily seen in domestic violence cases.

To be aware means, you need to know. You cannot know if you have not learned. We now live in a much more open society. Are women more independent than they were years ago? No. We now live in a society where that independence is more widely accepted. Some may disagree with that. Think back. Many years back a woman ran the household, paid the bills, took care of finances, and more. Is that not a form of independence? Do you think that being a single parent is a new concept? Isn't that a form of being independent? Do not confuse independence with equality. Today, women are more of an EQUAL than years past. There is a difference. Independence comes with a price. Never be so independent that you feel you do not need anyone. In general, men and women are a species that desire companionship. If someone believes or acts as though they do not need anyone; a relationship is not for them, and will never work. People need to be as independent of each other as they are dependent on one another. It comes down to balance. Equality also comes with a price. A woman cannot claim they should be able to do something then use the excuse they are a woman when they cannot perform the task. It is a great cause, and I fully support it. However, know your limitations. When you exceed them and fail, you are only hurting your cause. As much as the primary focus of this book regards what a woman fears are and why, we cannot turn our heads when the roles are reversed. Let us not beat a dead horse and move on. You may ask, what do I look for? There are signs you could watch for. Remember I stated earlier, in the beginning, everyone is on their best behavior. Those that act their normal self from the start are the exception, not the rule. Often times these changes are subtle and happen over time. Many times most will miss it because it is precise and difficult to analyze. Look at a few:

- Easily gets angry,
- Poor communicator,
- Self-centered; everything is about their needs, not yours,
- Verbally abusive, this can lead to physical abuse,
- Humiliates you in private or public,
- Grabs or pushes you, which can lead to greater physical violence,
- Verbally abusive or insulting,
- Mood swings,
- Very controlling,

- Always blaming you and not taking responsibility,
- Manipulates you or a situation,

These are the more common. However, there can be more or a variation of any or all of these. Also, someone can exhibit more than one of these signs at the same time. Removing the day-to-day life stresses from the equation, anytime you have to say to yourself, *'things will get better, he promised."* You are probably near, or in the early stages of an abusive relationship. The longer you allow this behavior, or enable this behavior, the worse it will get. The tricky part is if you wait too long to address it, it can escalate the situation and make it worse. At the first sign of these traits, they should be addressed, as well as your concerns, and resolved. Anything recognized and handled early, has a much better chance of being resolved and not getting worse. The longer you wait, the harder it becomes, especially if the situation is getting more volatile.

How do we approach this type of conversation? Now there is the number one question. Do you remember the human condition we talked about? This is what you always need to keep in mind. Whenever, even you, a person is accused of something, they WILL become defensive. Once that happens, you are wasting your words. That person will want to defend himself or herself. Some will do it by making excuses. Others may do it by trying to reverse the tide, meaning, putting you on the defensive by placing the blame on you. With this, you become on the defensive, the merry-go-round keeps turning, and no one ever gets off. What was resolved … nothing. Did it get worse … yes? So what is the answer? Actually, that is easier than you might think … if you can do it. NEVER make an accusation. When you accuse someone of something, the implication is; you feel they are guilty. That might very well be. However, that starts the defensive ball rolling. Does this make sense so far?

The best way to approach this by showing compassion and suggesting, by your questions, you are concerned about their well-being. For example; If my partner was verbally abusing me, those two approached might start like this.

"We need to talk. Why the heck are you treating me like shit?"

How does that sound to you? How would you answer that question? Or,

"Honey, is everything alright? Lately, you don't seem to be yourself."

This opens up a completely different door. Now that person will be open to listen and ask a question. Maybe, such as, I do not know what you mean. Give me an example."

Off you go to the races. No one is on the defensive … yet. This can easily end up being a constructive conversation. Do not always look to resolve everything in one conversation. Your position in this conversation is making the other individual see your perception of something. There are many techniques and ways to achieve this. I could write a book just on those. What I recommend is if you have a problem, or do not know how to approach it, it might be some time to get professional advice. Many couples cannot achieve this level of communications. They need someone to act as a mediator. In that case, it should be a professional, not a friend or family member. Friends and family take sides. A neutral party does not.

There are no magic pill that someone can take that will teach them how to communicate. It is a learned behavior, and you may not know everything about their past that makes this a difficult task. This particular section refers to men, women, same-sex marriages or relationships, or simply you as a person. Good communications skills are difficult to develop. It takes time. However, the rewards are plentiful. I said this earlier, and in many of my self-help books, people in general, suffer from a lack of knowing how to communicate. People will also tend to look at the effect that some has on them, and not look at how things affect someone else. A woman who was married for eighteen years was the victim of a sexual assault. Due to the nature of her husband's business, he would not let her report it. She wanted to. As she told her story, she was explaining how every attempt to talk to him about resulted in an argument or he would just say, "I don't want to discuss it," and walk away. She went to a counselor to discuss this because it was affecting their marriage. Her husband also refused to go with her. She mentioned that the counselor spoke to her about looking at the bigger picture. Was it possible that his denial was based around the fact that he could not accept the fact that it happened as well as being concerned for his business? The intimate part of their marriage, which had always been fine, had now decreased to be almost non-existent. She felt as if her husband was viewing her as something dirty.

She and the counselor discussed many things. To my point, the result was she reached a point where she had enough. She felt as if their marriage was over. They reached a point where they even stopped talking. All of this developed about seven months after the incident. She filed for divorce, which was something her husband did not want. He did agree to go to counseling with her. As she went on to explain, there were other issues besides his business, which in fact, he was using as an excuse. In one sense, he was selfish. Remember what I mentioned earlier; each person will react differently. That does not just apply to the victims; it applies to those around them as well. In his case, he would not discuss it because he could not handle the thought of went she went through and blamed himself that he was not there to protect her. In his eyes, to forget it and walk away was the way to solve it. Unfortunately, it is not. It only leads to deeper problems. In this case, they were lucky. They managed to be able to talk about it through their counselor and work it out. They did not get divorced. In cases such as these, that is a rare outcome. She shared her story with the hopes of helping anyone else going through the same thing.

The moral being, everyone is a victim. Yes, the victim carries the most weight. However, the effect goes further and deeper. The pain of these events does not cause people to look at it through the eyes of others. All they see and feel is their own pain. This is why professional help is so important in these cases. We all know that running from the truth is many times easier than facing it, but facing it is the only way to accept it. No woman has ever said, I was sexually assaulted, but it really did not happen.

CHAPTER 5

PREVENTION

How does a woman prevent herself from being abused? That is the million-dollar question. First, there is no 100% guarantee because no one can control the actions of another. What a woman can do is drastically reduce the risks.

- **Do your homework.**

Many say dating sites are the way to go. You have a chance to screen someone before you talk to them or meet them. Is that true? There are those that are honest, and many more that are not. There are many fake people. How many times have you heard on the news of an assault on a woman by someone she met on a dating site? When you look at the number of people who use dating sites and compare that to those instances, yes, and the percentage is small, but then, how many are actually reported? I used a dating site once. My experience was every person states they exercise 3-5 times per week. They all travel. They all ski and play golf. They are all passionate and caring. The best one is; all their photos are recent. Look, I am not knocking dating sites. Everyone posts what they think may be attractive to someone else rather than just be honest about themselves. Do not rush out there. Talk on the phone first. Get a feel for the person. Get their name. Google them and see if they are for real. A female friend of mine spends the money to run a background search on anyone she is going to date. That is a personal preference. My point is, you need to be pro-active in finding out about the person. Do not meet them in a dark parking lot to go somewhere. Meet them where you are going to meet, somewhere that is public.

- **Use your experience**

You have been with men before. Use your experience. Listen to yourself. If something does not feel it, it probably is not. Do not let a few bucks in someone's pocket, a fancy car, or good looks fool you. Every person wants a partner they are attracted to, and someone who is financially secure. However, do not let that blind you. Those things are all superficial. The richest thing someone may offer is what is in their heart.

- **Watch for the signs**

A person can only put up a front for so long. Watch them. Watch their moves, how they speak to your server if you are in a restaurant. Watch how they interact with others, especially you. As you are talking, and you should be, you may hit on a sensitive subject. How do they react? Any signs of anger this early on is NEVER good. It is a red flag. Do they listen, or just like to talk? Are they constantly changing the subject? Do they seem relaxed? There will only be a bit of nervousness for the first few minutes. That should go away. Ask questions. Anyone that is not willing to answer your questions or takes too long to reply might be hiding something. My father used to say always tell the truth. You never have to remember the truth, a lie you have to remember forever. Read some articles on human characteristics. You know if the type of question you are asking should be something they should know versus what they might have to think about. It takes time to get to know someone. If you rush, you are missing the joys of exploration, and increasing your risks. In the beginning, everyone, yes even you, are on your best behavior. It takes time for people to settle in and be relaxed. It also takes months, and maybe years before you know all aspects of a person. You do not have to wait that long. There is no preset defined period. You will know when you have reached that point.

- **Don't take it**

If something that occurs, that concerns you, no matter how minor. Address it before it becomes an issue. Keep in mind what we spoke of earlier. The vast majority of female abuse cases started with smaller things that eventually got worse. You are not going to marry or live with this person tomorrow. Now is the time to address these matters. The time when walking away is the easiest. If you are with someone who treats others badly, most likely at some point they will do that to you.

- **Know yourself**

The largest mistake people make is either not knowing themselves or settling. No one is perfect. The key is to be able to see if you can live with someone else's imperfections. A large part of not settling involves your degree of self-worth and self-respect. Know how you want to be treated, and command that respect. Not in a mean or bad way, in a way that correctly expresses your expectations.

- **Communicate**

Everything starts and ends with strong communication skills, between all parties. Some people can explain things better than others can or are more talkative than others are. The important factor is that you communicate, and at the end of the conversation, the proper message was received and UNDERSTOOD. Never assume that someone understands what you said. You may have said in a manner how you perceived it, and the other person perceived it differently. Be sure your message is clear. Also, be sure you understand the other person's message.

- **Listen as well as you speak**

For any communication to be effective, each person MUST be able to see the issue through the eyes of the other person. If not, it will always be an "agree to disagree" conversation, and the issue will never be resolved. It will live to haunt you another day. The problem with that scenario is each day the issue will become worse and become more volatile. Figure out what it takes to make your method of communicating work.

As you can see, prevention is a multi-tier system. I was married to a Gal that was very independent. I respected that. However, she was so independent she felt she could dress any way she chose to, and people should respect that. THIS IS NOT THE CASE. In a perfect world, women should be able to wear something suggestive without worry of receiving suggestive comments and being stared upon my men. In a perfect world, no one should have to carry a gun because people would not commit crimes. In a perfect world, a woman should not have to carry a legal taser or pepper spray to protect herself. In a perfect world, a woman should take martial arts courses because they enjoy the art, not for protection. In a perfect world, a woman wearing a wedding band should be hit on by any man. Do we live in this perfect world? Does it exist? Absolutely not. My ex-wife was a beautiful woman. I can't tell you how many times we were out and if I left to go to the restroom, on my way back I would see a man leaving the table, just to find out that they tried to introduce themselves. I mean really, unless someone is blind, did they not see me sitting there before I left. On one occasion, the same man did this two or three times. This caused me to have to confront him about this, which led to further things. It did not end well. For him that is.

There is being independent, and there is being realistic. If a woman wants to be aware, she must be aware of reality, regardless of how she feels about her independence. Many of these minor occurrences are innocent. However, many are not. They are a test for someone to see how far they can take something. What can they get away with and will they get lucky? Far too many times, I have seen women end up in an uncomfortable situation because they were trying to be polite. Today, no one knows the type of person they are dealing with. When I was younger and did the club scene, there were times I approached a woman and did not realize that until I introduced myself, she was married. Once I found out, that was it.

Many men will come back for more attempts. I said earlier, I used to work at a nightclub. One night this type of occurrence happened. A few married women out for a few drinks. One man kept bothering this one woman. She did not come to the management or me. Had she, we would have asked him to leave. She and her friends decided it was best to leave. Someone came in to report a man was bothering a woman in the parking lot. Of course, I and someone else went outside. Sure enough, he followed them out to continue to try to get to this woman. We called the police, restrained him, and he was arrested. What might have happened if she had been alone and not with friends? Someone can become fixated on someone due to the challenge. It can become an obsession for them. They might follow them home, find out their address, or assault them on the way. How many cases of carjacking's have you seen on the news? I have spoken to women who have had these experiences and were raped during the process. I have responded to medical calls for this same type of occurrence.

We cannot just do what we want without taking some precautions. The days of sitting around at night with your front door open and unlocked are over. NEVER let your independence of thought and actions outweigh your need for AWARENESS and PREVENTION. There are those in this world that suffer from different forms of mental disorders, some are sexual. You have an obligation to yourself as well as those who love you to be aware of this and make the necessary adjustments to reduce your risk. It is like going shopping at night and parking your car. What woman would ever park her car in a dark area of a parking lot at night, versus closer to a lighted area? Yet, you see it all the time. No, you are not literally asking for trouble, but you are certainly not taking all the precautions to avoid it. We live in a hurried and rushed world. Everything needs to be done yesterday, or we just want to do it and get it out of the way. Therefore, we do not think. We simply act. This speaks to the conscious versus sub-conscious thought process we talked about earlier. The things that are important to your safety should become learned behaviors. You do not have to like them; you only have to practice them. By doing this, you do not always need to rely on your conscious mind since it will become a habit. Much of this should be practiced by men as well, but they are at a much lower risk. At night, who is more likely to be assaulted or mugged in a parking lot; would it a 6'4" 210-pound man, or a 5'4" woman weighing 120 pounds? This is not a gender thing. This is simply truth and reality.

This is part of preventative thinking. Preventive thinking and awareness go hand in hand. Remember this simple rule. ***"If it doesn't feel right, it probably is not right."*** Preventative thinking and awareness are a woman's greatest tools. There are multiple other ways you can display your independence. Speaking of independence, is being independent a state of mind, or something you need to prove? In general, most people feel as if they have to prove themselves. They do this by any means. Attire is a form of making your personal statement. However, is it possible that your personal statement can be made verbally? If you engaged in a conversation, you certainly could make your independence known by what you say, how you say it, and how you present it. Yes, saying it and presenting it are completely different. Words alone do not always send a message. It also has to do with how you say them. When we are not engaged in conversation, people sum up us up by what they see. When someone looks at you, ask yourself, *what type of perception do I want people to have of me?* Perception perceived is perception achieved. When you get right down to it, men and women both flirt. In most cases, they are writing checks they are not prepared to have cashed. Meaning, if you do not want to be looked upon as an "easy mark," then do not dress or act like one. I am not trying to be insulting. This is a fact, one that can lead to a painful and emotional damaging experience.

I have seen it all. I have seen abuse in every form. In domestic violence situations, it is most commonly due to a man who is a creep. Suffers from past issues, or has a huge insecurity and inferiority complex. However, in an unattached relationship, it is always something that triggered the event. In the case of a man with a mental disorder, you never know who that will be, and what could trigger them. You MUST reduce your risks if you want to reduce that chance of becoming a victim. Therefore, I ask you. What is more important? You need to display your female independence, or your safety, and possibly your life. I have heard countless stories from women who have said, "I carry mace. I used it, and it didn't stop him." We also live in a world of substance abuse. Any form of substance abuse can alter the effects of any deterring tool. I have seen people on drugs that were tased multiple times by people and kept coming. There are documented cases of individuals being shot and kept coming at a person. That can be frightening, and it should be. That is exactly what I am trying to do. Scar the shit out of you because that threat is real.

I am saying you should be dressing in a manner that you are covered from your forehead to your ankles; of course not. However, answer me this. Why is it some women have the need to dress so provocatively that half of their breasts are exposed, or if they bend over their skirt or dress is so short, that you can see whether they are wearing panties or not? What I referring to when it comes to prevention is moderation. You are not a movie star posing for photos at a red carpet event surrounded by security. You are out in the everyday world. A world that dictates you should be more careful. Remember what I said. There is no excuse for abuse in any form. However, we have a conscious responsibility to know what we are faced with and should try to avoid it AT ALL COSTS. Women that have been raped will tell you they know it is was not their fault. However, that knowledge does not take away for the physical and emotional trauma they went through or made the healing process any easier. The other argument I have heard is, "I took self-defense lessons." Here is another truth. That may help you in a one-on-one situation, which is very view. In these cases, there are often multiple assailants. Basic self-defense training will not help you here. I have also spoken with women who carry a firearm. Whether you agree or disagree with it is not the question. The fact is, when this happens, it is completely unexpected, and you may not have time to get at your firearm. You also now have the risk that the firearm could be taken from you and used against you.

By now, I am positive you are saying to yourself, *"I can't just stay home all the time."* You are correct. You cannot, but you can take precautions and study up on awareness and prevention. Most importantly, be prepared to implement those concepts. Do not be that woman who sits and watches the news and says, *"That will never happen to me."* Keep in mind if it never happened to anyone, there would be no reason for me, and other authors to write these books. It does happen, and to real people; people such as yourself. Do not be a victim. Knowledge is power. Be informed, and make the correct choices. Life stinks at times. No matter what we do, we can do it right. Correct in every way, yet still, it will have a bad outcome. The risk of you driving your car into a bridge abutment is far less if you are driving sober than it is if you are under some form of substance abuse. As we discuss this next point, you will see how this ties together. Many of you may say, *"I already know all of this."* You may.

However, they are not at the forefront of your thoughts. Much of this you know sits in your sub-conscious mind. The human condition dictates that people are creatures of habit. Meaning, if something is not a habit, you do not do it. If you do not get into the habit of making your bed in the morning, you will come home to a messy bed every day. Once it becomes a habit, it becomes muscle memory, and you come home to a made bed every day. This concept applies to every aspect of your life, regardless of the analogy I use. Prevention and awareness have to become muscle memory. Your knowledge must be moved from your subconscious mind to your conscious mind, meaning, once you are always thinking about it, it will become a muscle memory habit, and you will no longer need to think about it. Similar to putting your car keys in the same place every time you walk into your house. At first, to learn to do this, you must think about every day. Eventually, it will become a habit, and you will do it automatically. Therefore, no further thought will be needed. What is the keyword we are referring to?

THINKING - is the process of using one's mind to consider or reason about something. That has a wide range, as it should. It applies to everything you do. As an example, a woman I met at a meeting said to me, *"After listening to my husband complain about what I wear, and after my attempted rape, I realized he was* *right, and after a while I found myself buying different types of clothes."* This woman was very fortunate. She was a victim of an attempted rape that was broken up by bystanders. The assailant was restrained by two men, and arrested by the police when they arrived. As it turned out, he had a mental disorder, and this was not his first offense. She admitted that she never wore short dresses or skirts, but did wear very revealing tops, and very tight shirts. She had breast implant a few years back and enjoyed seeing how nice she looked. I get it. We all have a degree of vanity in us. Do you think for one minute because I am a man there is a certain degree of vanity in me? If you think that, you are sadly mistaken. Every person has a degree of vanity within him or her. The only difference being, some act on it at some level, and others do not.

Thinking is a process. The first step in that process requires that the person be honest with himself or herself. You can lie to me but never lie to yourself. If you do, the thinking process will be skewed; therefore, your outcome or resolution will be skewed as well. Like any mathematical equation, the answer will only be as accurate as the data that is put into the equation. One of the hardest physiologic things for any person to do is, to be honest with themselves. Do you know why? The reason is that the vast majority of your time is spent defending yourself and justifying what or why you did something or acted a particular way. Most of this originates at the workplace. Eventually, we make excuses for what we did for our minds to justify our actions. The only way to overcome this part of the human condition, and become a truthful and honest person to others as well as yourself, is, to be honest with yourself first. That is where it all starts. At the basic level of thinking stage in your brain. If you cannot be honest with yourself, you will never be honest with anyone. You will spend your life making excuses.

I hope you can see how the process of thinking ties everything together. Here are some of the excuses people use during their thinking process:

- I should be able to do what I want,
- If it wasn't for ...
- It is all their fault,

- I wanted to do it that way but ….,
- No one can tell me what to do,
- Don't tell me what to do,
- Who do you think you are?
- I may be your (wife, partner, girlfriend, etc.), but am I still my own person,
- I am going to do what I want to do.

Read them again and tell me; do any of these statements sound familiar? They should because, at some point in time, everyone has used them. The psychological effect is although you may have used them and justified their use, when you read them, they sound self-centered. Why is that? The answer is, they are self-centered. That does not make you a bad person. It makes you human. When people try to justify anything they do, they do not view it as being self-centered because it is personal. It involves them on a deeply personal level. However, they will pass judgment on others that have done the same thing. There is it. That human condition again. Why are phycologists and therapists so successful? They understand the one thing that others do not. They understand the human condition. What does that have to do with forms of abuse? It has everything to do with it. Let us quickly break it down.

The human condition is defined as "the characteristics, key events, and situations which compose the essentials of human existence, such as birth, growth, emotionality, aspiration, conflict, and mortality." This is a very broad topic, which has been and continues to be pondered and analyzed from many perspectives, including those of religion, philosophy, history, art, literature, anthropology, psychology, and biology.

As you can see, it encompasses a great deal, and by definition alone, you should be able to see that it involves every aspect of a person's life. The tricky part is, the human condition for each person varies slightly. Some things are innate, meaning, hardwired into them since birth and embedded in their DNA. The rest are learned behaviors. Learned behaviors are much easier to change. However, both can be changed if someone really wants to, which leads us to acceptance and enabling. Any time you accept behavior from a partner that you feel is abuse, you are allowing it to continue by enabling them not to have to stop. Why do women do this? It goes back to the many reasons I mentioned earlier, the most common being some type of fear. Fear of being alone, losing the man, being a single parent, and more. FEAR is the number one reason why domestic abuse continues.

As you can see, part of prevention is awareness, and part of awareness is prevention. One goes with the other. You cannot prevent something you are not aware of, and you cannot be aware of it without trying to prevent it. The most difficult part of this topic is that most women do not want to think about the possibility that some form of abuse can happen to them. The same holds true for anything in our lives we do not want to happen to us. We simply do not think about it. Ignorance of any possibility is not awareness, nor prevention. It is ignorance. We know it exists, we choose to ignore it. Those women are the most vulnerable because they trust. Nothing is wrong with trust. Actually, trust is healthy and a necessity; does that sound contradictory? Do not confuse trusting your partner with trusting the world around you. I stated earlier that domestic violence is the number one cause of female abuse. Can you trust and not trust at the same time? Do you need to? Neither of those two questions is relevant. In a relationship, trust develops over time. During that time, a woman needs to evaluate her potential partner. No one completely trusts anyone right out of the gate. It is no different for a man. When I start to date someone, I look for signs in their behavior. That does not mean I do not enjoy their company or have a nice time. It simply means I am looking for things that make us compatible. As a man, and like most men, I do not worry about a woman physically abusing me. Emotional abuse is a different subject. Emotional abuse is a wide term and encompasses many things. Things that are different for each individual. Some women do not mind MILD sexual comments or suggestions. Others do. Both men and women use sex as a tool. A man may threaten to get it somewhere else, a woman may use it as a tool to get what she wants, or use it as a form of punishment. These are all very dangerous games to play with your partner.

A woman can only tell a man to get it somewhere else so many times before he will do just that. A man can verbally, or emotionally, abuse his partner so many times before she will find comfort somewhere else. I mentioned when I was younger I worked as a bouncer. The door attendant that trained me, oh yes; there is training. Most people think a bouncer's job is to beat people up and throw people out. Although that may be part of it, it is a small part of it. The largest part is watching people, getting to know people's habits to stop a problem before it happens. With that said, this person that was training me said, I don't care if a woman is married, dating someone, or single. Given the right set of circumstances at the right time, anyone can cheat. Now that some woman's hair is stating up do not take that as an insult. Many will say I would never cheat on my husband or boyfriend. Under normal circumstances, you are probably correct. Never judge what you may or may not do until you are in that position. I have seen friends I never thought would be unfaithful be just that. Later to find out all the emotional abuse they went through. They reached a point that they felt so down about themselves they needed for someone, anyone, to make them feel special. Hey … you don't have to agree. We can agree to disagree. However, the one thing I may have over you is all that I have seen during my professional medical career. When I tell you it happens, it does, and far more than you think. Remember, I spoke to this earlier. Take a review of the facts. I also gave you the website reference for this. In case you did not write it down, here it is again. *https://www.trustify.info/ blog/infidelity-statistics-2017.*

Infidelity Statistics

- In over 1/3 of marriages, one or both partners admit to cheating.
- 22% of men say that they have cheated on their significant other.
- 14% of women admit to cheating on their significant other.
- 36% of men and women admit to having an affair with a coworker.
- 17% of men and women admit to having an affair with a sister-in-law or brother-in-law.

- People who have cheated before are 350% more likely to cheat again.
- Affairs are most likely to occur two years into a marriage.
- 35% of men and women admit to cheating while on a business trip.
- 9% of men admit they might have an affair to get back at a spouse.
- 14% of women admit they might have an affair to get back at a spouse.
- 10% of affairs begin online.
- 40% of the time online affairs turn into real life affairs.

Why are these numbers so staggering? Some just like the challenge and not get caught. Some of it is a personal emotional problem. The majority of it comes from some form of emotional abuse. People needing to get what they need, they are not getting at home, or from their partner. It is also due to the ease, availability, and opportunity. I once said the only difference between a child and an adult is the way they think. A child is innocent. They think in black and white. To an adult, there are many greys areas, and they think in color. Those grey areas are the areas that make adults do what they do. Ease, availability, and opportunity.

Sexual harassment and advances are quite popular in schools and colleges now. Why is that? A teacher or professor might feel no one would say anything because who would believe them. Student's grades may not be what they need to be. A suggestion is made, and well, you hear it on the news. At times, this comes out years later. As I stated earlier, very few will stand up alone. However, once one takes that step, others that were abused or harassed will step up. That has always been a problem with our society. As a society, people are quick to judge others; therefore, victims do not speak out. Yes, it has gotten better but has a long way to go. How difficult do you think it is for a young girl who has been raped? She may never be known as her first name, rather, she will be known as the girl who was raped. The main reason why when this occurs, people move. Get away from the area where this occurred. Give their child a fresh start. All of this because of the way society judges. When I refer to society, I am NOT pointing the finger at you. I am referring to society as a whole. The general concept of what MOST people do.

At the very least, this is a major issue. It causes the people who are doing these things to be able to continue. It goes on for years. It is estimated that close to 80% of child maltreatment fatalities involve at least one parent of the perpetrator. The American Society of Positive Care for Children posted these statistics. Their hotline number is 1-800-656-HOPE:

SEXUAL ABUSE STATISTICS

- 1 in 4 girls and 1 in 6 boys will be sexually abused before they turn 18 years old.
- Over 58,000 children were sexually abused last year.
- 8.3 % of reported child abuse cases were sexual abuse.
- 34% of people who sexually abuse a child are family members.
- 12.3% of girls were age 10 or younger at the time of their first rape/victimization, and 30% of girls were between the ages of 11 and 17.
- 27.8% of boys were age 10 or younger at the time of their first rape/victimization.
- 96% of people who sexually abuse children are male, and 76.8% of people who sexually abuse children are adults.
- 325,000 children are at risk of becoming victims of commercial child sexual exploitation each year.
- Caregiver alcohol or drug abuse is a child abuse risk factor putting kids at much higher risk of being abused.
- The average age at which girls first become victims of prostitution is 12 to 14 years old, and the average age for boys is 11 to 13 years old.

That is just too frightening, and just represents the cases that were either reported or found out about through other means. It is estimated that every 98 seconds an American is sexually assaulted in some form. Ages 12-34 are the highest risk years for rape and sexual assault. Those under the age of 65 are 92% less likely to be victims of rape or sexual assault compared to the ages of 12-34, and

84% less likely than the 25-49 age group. Keep in mind; this is a reflection of reported cases. How many do you think are NEVER reported? Like all studies, the numbers and percentages will vary from site to site, or study to study depending on the criteria used. Look at these figures as approximate percentages. Even at that, they are alarming. This why awareness leads to prevention and is so important. Before we move on to the next chapter, let me leave you with this story.

I met a woman during a counseling session who was not there because of anything that happened to her. She was there trying to cope with what had happened to her daughter. Her daughter was seeing a therapist after being raped at the age of fifteen. Since that time, she could not have a relationship and continued to suffer from nightmares of the event. She was now twenty-two years old. Her mother was also having problems coping with this because her daughter did not appear to get any better. She needed help to cope with this and help her daughter. As the story goes, this young girl had a brother that was two years older than her daughter was. As best as I could determine, he was not well liked in high school and never had any dates, or went to his proms. He had few friends. One night her parents were out to dinner. Her brother was home with a friend playing video games. She was going to take a shower before she went over to a friend's house to work on a school project. After she showered, her brother and his friend raped her and left the house. They threatened her that if she told, they would do it again. As it turned out, her brother had a history of peeking in on her when she was in the shower. She caught him many times. One time, she could him masturbating while he watched her shower. She would tell him never to watch her again. The bathroom door had the old fashion lock on it that with a paper clip, you could unlock the door from the outside. He promised he would not do it again. She never told her parents. This was not an everyday occurrence and only happened three or four times throughout a year. She did not want to get her brother in trouble.

Think about this story and try to figure out all the reasons this got to this point. Part of the reason this mother was going to these sessions was that she and her husband never saw the signs building up in their son. You always need to be AWARE. That is a very vulnerable age. Everyone wants to be accepted, their hormones are raging, and somewhere along the line, the parents felt they missed his deeper issues. How many factors can you think of?

CHAPTER 6

THE EFFECTS

So far, we have covered a tremendous amount of information in this book, and I have shared many stories. The story that affected me personally is still yet to come. When we speak of effects, we must understand the degree will vary for each woman. This is a result of many factors. Emotional development, experience, environment, upbringing, age, and experiences, all play a role in how a traumatic event such as abuse will affect them. Although something may seem harmless to you, it could have a devastating effect on another. All forms of abuse can have a short or long-term effect on its victims. Certainly, many of the minor offensives are often times forgotten in minutes. We are not referring to those. The following are some of the effects someone can suffer from:

- Depression or suicidal thoughts,
- Lead to alcoholism or drug use,
- Increases the risk of sexually transmitted diseases, or pregnancy,
- It can affect family, relationships, friendships, work,
- Embarrassment causes many of these not to be reported,
- Become introverted, meaning, they withdrawn from their surroundings or society,

These are just a few of the most common ones. Keep in mind, each person will react differently. Embarrassment and shame come first. Most will not want to talk about it. Eventually, anger sets in. These two stages can last for a long time. At some point, the hope is a victim seeks counseling and eventually reached a point of acceptance. Do not confuse acceptance with approval. Acceptance means they can accept what has happened and start to move forward with their life. There are many documented cases when a victim of a sexual assault finds it very difficult to move on, it affects their marriage to a point where divorce can occur. This form of abuse can be life-altering in many aspects. Usually, both partners are engaged with counseling. There are also men that cannot get over the event and alienate their spouse. This causes increasing distress and severely hinders their ability to get past it. There are many websites available to view all the psychological effects of this type of abuse because I can write a separate book just on that topic. It is sad to say in most cases, the victim's lives may never be the same. Anything can trigger the memory. Yelling, seeing an abuse scene on TV or in a movie theatre, reading a scene in a book, or hearing something on the news, can all be triggers that cause a victim to relive their experience.

Often times in children, the effect may not manifest for years. Depending on the age of their abuse, they may not really understand it until years later. I believe I mentioned a story of a woman who was sexually abused as a child. The effects of this did not manifest until she was in her second year of marriage. They had no children at the time, and sadly, this situation ended n a divorce. In a perfect world, a partner would understand this and give that person as much time as they needed. Unfortunately, we do not live in a perfect world. Therefore, a person's degree of understanding and patience will vary. Does that make them bad people, or does it make them who they are? Is judging those who cannot handle it the same as those that judge the victims? Is judging anyone right or wrong? These questions you have to answer for yourself. One of the issues that arise from people judging others is that they are doing based on what they think they would do. Is that a fair judgment, or should people for an OPINION based on the facts and understanding the human condition, which in most cases, people will not agree with. No one can actually say what they would do, or how they would react. This is the reason why people need to be objective, and not subjective.

Effects can lead to deeper issues as they affect someone's daily life. They can cause many underlying issues that someone is not consciously aware of, but their reactions can be based on these underlying issues. Issues such as anger, being short-tempered, judgmental, and less understanding, are just some of the underlying issues. What complicates things further is the victim is not aware they are this way, and they will become very defensive when these things are pointed out. Anger is a like a self-momentum engine. It fuels itself. As it gets more fuel, it escalates and moves along much quicker as it builds up speed. Not many have the patience to sit back, keep their mouth shut, and be supportive. Part of any emotional healing process involves releasing that anger and letting it go. Carrying it, or suppressing it only leads to greater, and sometimes more dangerous and volatile issues. This is why support groups are so important. It is a safe place. A place to vent, and get things emotions out into the open, which is much easier to do with others that have gone through it, are going through it, and understand the frustration. This should only be accomplished in a controlled environment, meaning, in the presence of a counselor that can defuse a situation when necessary.

Look at it from this viewpoint. Picture yourself paralyzed. You cannot move, and you cannot speak, but you want to. I have seen that look on so many women's face in support groups. You can tell they want to tell their story, but simply cannot. No one can force them, and no one should. They need to do that when they are ready, and that time varies from woman to woman. Remember what I mentioned earlier, it is not necessarily the event that happened as much as it is the effect that event had on that person. One evening, a woman who was in a physically abusive marriage was telling her story. Her depression was not as much due to the physical abuse aspect as much as it was that she went back to her husband four times before she finally left for good. The data shows that in general, a woman will go back to an abusive relationship an average of seven times before she finally leaves for good. That number is dependent on many factors.

- How long in-between the events
- Finances

- Children
- Self-respect or low esteem

In almost every cases, physical abuse in a relationship also cases emotional abuse. The woman may now have low self-esteem or respect. She may feel that no one will want her, and she has no self-worth. Therefore, they will go back. This is one of the most dangerous situations because the individual causes the abuse feels more confident each time she comes back, which can lead to more severe forms of physical abuse. Have no doubts. This complex subject has a multitude of psychological effects. All of which can determine a positive or negative outcome. As with most things, early detective and getting help greatly increases the chance of a positive outcome. Everyone perceives a positive outcome differently. Some feel a positive outcome is a result of the woman finally leaving for good. Someone else may perceive it as the situation gets resolved, and everyone lives happily ever after. My view of a positive outcome is basic. ***An outcome is positive when the result is what is best for the situation.*** This is totally inclusive of all aspect of the problem. Everyone likes the fairy tale ending, which is perceived as everyone stays together and loves eternally. We get that perception from the movies. The reality is, a fairytale ending is when everything works out for all parties. They are now happy and can move on, regardless of what that takes. That is the reality of the real world, not the movie world.

Any change from the norm is difficult. People find it hard to change because they fail to embrace change. The unknown scares them. However, in every physical domestic violence abuse case, CHANGE MUST OCCUR. A person can face that or fear it, and it takes time. Have you ever wondered why some people can just pick up and move to another state, not knowing anyone, having no specific contacts, and maybe not even having a job? Does this mean they do not have a fear of change? Not at all, but what they do have is a willingness to embraces it, and know this is a step to something that might be better. That is called courage. It takes a great deal of courage for any woman to face what she has experienced, as well as the road she will need to travel to overcome it. We are creatures of habit and comfort. A police officer friend of mine once told me, they do not worry about the everyday citizen.

They can find them anytime because they have the same routine. They take the same route to work, stop at the same coffee shop, or shop at the same store. They are easy to find. The criminal varies their routine; which makes this become a greater challenge. One of the things all police departments teach is not to be routine. Take different routes to work on different says. Do not always shop at the same store, or get your coffee from the same place. If you are stalked by some sicko, this makes it more difficult and in many cases, they will move on. Before any woman even puts on her seatbelt, she should lock the car doors. Always look around you when you are walking to your car. Know your surroundings. A remote device that unlocks a car door saves valuable seconds where you do not have to try to get your key in the lock. Have your keys out and ready. You do not want to stand outside your car for minutes searching through your pocketbook to find your keys. These are more examples of PREVENTION and COMMON SENSE things that can save your life.

Part of realizing the effects is gaining the knowledge to help you prevent experiencing those effects and becoming a victim. During daylight hours, there are many people in a busy supermarket parking. The risks are greatly reduced. However, many women like to shop at night when the stores are less busy. I know a woman that leaves her carriage inside and a clerk watches it. She gets her car, drives up to the well-lit front of the store, brings out her shopping cart, and loads her car. Does that seem a little overboard to you? Some may say yes. I say not at all. I call it smart. Since she rather go to the store at night, she is taking the proper precautions. Never allow anyone to criticize you for taking the proper safety precautions. As unfortunate as it may seem, the world is such that we must all think ahead of what we are doing. To dig a bit deeper regarding the effect of these traumatic events, they are systemic. Meaning, the effects on family, child, and others can be just as devastating. Yes, in a different way, but everyone shares in the emotional trauma. When a sexual assault occurs, or other types of physical violence, it is a normal response for a woman to become very protective. That protectiveness extends to everything in her life. Children do not understand the changes mommy is going through, and her partner must exercise a great deal of caution to what he says, how he says it, and even how he approached her. Even if it just to give her a hug or a kiss on the cheek to display understanding. Some women have stated they could not let their husbands sleep in their bed. An innocent touch in the middle of the night would set them off. This is described as the systemic effect. It affects the entire living system. I have said this before, and I will make sure this message hits home. Early counseling is paramount. No man will ever understand the complexity of the emotional distress a woman feels if they are sexually abused or assaulted by a stranger, partner, or a family member. It is a personal violation on every level. I have witnessed women telling their story as they sit and shake uncontrollably in their chair.

As a paramedic, I spent limited time with victims while caring for them. My heart broke to see what they experienced, along with knowing the road they face ahead. Female, and yes, male counselors deserve to be saints. When I leave a group meeting with these women, I feel the emotional effects for days. To call them women or a woman seems so impersonal. They all have names. However, I cannot and would never speak about them by name. Things in life we do not like to think about we tend not to think about. When you are in the healthcare field, you do not have that luxury. You seem you face it, and you MUST deal with it. As they speak, they look at the floor, not as a person. That is due to their degree of embarrassment. Something they should not feel embarrassed about, but they will. In time, they get better and look at others. Imagine being a woman, and living every waking moment in fear. Taking medications, you never had to take before to control your anxiety. Medications you may never be able to come off. Your life has been permanently changed, as have the lives of those around them. Once depression sets in, there is the feeling of hopelessness. There is no light at the end of the tunnel. We know there is, we know it can get better, but it is a long road. Keep in mind that everyone reacts differently.

Are there financial effects? Most households are two incomes, and many of them live paycheck to paycheck. It will be sometime before that individual is able to return to work. That adds financial stress to the situation. This requires a great deal of family support, which works for those who have family locally. For those that do not, this only adds to the stress of an already stressed situation. How far can that rubber band stretch before it breaks? These are many of the hidden stressors. The ones most people do not think about, but they exist. In life, no one expects the unexpected, but the unexpected happens. That statement does not only apply to female abuse, but it also applies to everything in life. We have spoken about many types of effects in this chapter. However, we have not yet spoken about what is the most immediate, after these events occur; the physical effects and the process.

PHYSICAL EFFECTS:

The physical effects will heal. Depending on the degree of injury, they may be completely unnoticeable or leave scars. Obviously, scars are the worst of the two because they are a constant reminder of what happened. Although people do not mean harm when they ask, many will ask if they see a scare, "How did you get that?" Every day a woman looks in a mirror and asks that question, they are reliving their horrible experience. We are not talking about someone who fell and scraped a knee. It heals, they forget it, and life goes on. Abuse is an event that is a lifelong memory. This memory is a wound that is opened many times for various reasons over their lifetime. Some of these may include:

- Looking in a mirror
- Someone asking a question
- See an abuse scene on TV or in a movie
- Hearing about it on the news
- Hearing about it happening to a friend or family member

These are just a few. My point being, that for those that have not experienced this trauma these are everyday occurrences that no one gives a second thought about on a daily basis except the woman who suffered from an abusive situation or sexual assault. The interesting thing about haring about something, or reading about it is, at times, the take-home message never makes it to the part of the brain that remembers it. The facts are, people are visually based. They remember more of what they see rather than what they hear or read about. As an example, we hear of police officers or other heroes that died in the line of duty. We do not remember that for long because all we see is the picture of a face, in a non-traumatic pose, versus, what that person looked like after the event. You will remember a dog that was struck and killed in a street that you drove by and witnessed much longer than you will remember the face of the fallen hero. The reason is you have a visual reference to it in your brain.

To bring a sense of reality this part of the topic, let me detail some of the injuries I have seen that women I have cared for sustained. I will let your mind draw its own pictures because frankly, some of these injuries you would not want to see.

- Eyes black and blue swollen to the point where they are completely shut
- Lips split wide open
- Teeth knocked out of their mouth
- Broken arms, hands, or wrists
- Gunshot wounds to various parts of the body
- Stab Wounds
- Gunshot Wounds
- Severe vaginal bleeding
- Hair pulled out from their head
- Bleeding from a variety of injuries
- Cigarette or other types of burns to their body
- Broken jaws

I could list even more, but I think you get my point.

EMOTIONAL EFFECTS:

- Confusion secondary to reflection
- Strategies on how to leave a bad situation
- Shame
- Pressure for sex with multiple partners

- Family relationships
- Leads to PTSD, mental health issues, a feeling of being controlled
- More …..

These effects of physical and emotional abuse are a direct result of violent and brutal crimes such as physical assault, or sexual assault. To bring reality to it, let us call it what it is. That word is RAPE. A word that is hideous and terrible. As a man, I despise watching a movie scene that display rape. I get it, it is a reality, and maybe a form of awareness that these things happen in the real world. It is just my preference because I know and have seen the reality of it. Before we move on, let me tell you what happens in the case of rape. If available, a description of the assailant is always the best form of evidence. However, in most cases, many will cover their face making this impossible. The woman is so terrified at the time, and fighting back, she is not she looking for things we call distinguishing marks such as a tattoo, a scar, or other markers that can identify the assailant. These are important because if that person was ever arrested in the past, their tattoo's, scars, or other distinguishing marks are noted in their record. This makes crossing referencing to a possible assailant(s) easier, and can narrow the field. Think about that for a moment. If you were ever in that situation, would you be thinking about doing that?

The data shows that every 98 seconds, someone is sexually assaulted in some form in the United States. Let us long at the process. First, the crime scene is completely secured. The first responders and medical personnel must take careful steps to preserve all evidence at the scene, as well as what must is transported to the hospital. Medical personnel such as I was, are specially trained in this task. In the immediate aftermath, the victim may choose or be asked to undergo a forensic examination to collect any evidence left behind by the attacker. Once the victim arrives at the hospital, a rape kit is used, and a rape kit exam is performed. Does that sound like the embarrassment of the event is over? I will add, the doctors and nurses are extremely conscious of privacy, and are so caring and understanding. They do all they can to make this as comfortable as possible under the circumstances.

A minimal number of people are on this team and are specially trained in this process.

I must state, that any or all parts of this examination can be declined at any point.

- First, a thorough medical history is obtained from the victim.
- They must stand on a large piece of paper while undressing so any evidence since as hair, or a fingernail or other fine items that may fall will be obtained.
- Everything is collected and tested for DNA.
- Any injuries are then documented and treated as needed. Any further evidence it collected.
- The examiner collects biological evidence such as saliva, blood, semen, urine, skin cells and hair by taking swabs of the victim's skins, genitalia, anus, and mouth.
- They will scrap under the victim's fingernails and combing through the victim's hair.
- The victim's body is photographed from head to toe to document on bruising or other injuries.
- Once the exam is complete, the evidence that was collected is carefully packaged and labeled to prevent contamination.

Does this sound like something anyone would want to undergo immediately after this type of attack? It sounds cruel and non-caring, but need to happen, so no possible evidence is lost. The sheet that the victim laid on, or was covered with, during transport in an ambulance is also turned into the hospital staff. Forensic science has come a long way. DNA of an assailant could be found in a scratch on the victim's body. This exam is a slow and painstaking task for everyone. Some may dislike that I have described so many things in details. However, I will accept the dislike if this book saves one woman from experiencing any of these things. These rape kits may vary from state to state.

Remember, woman, are often times afraid to report being raped because they are nervous about testifying in court, the embarrassment, and other factors. It is a known fact that defense attorneys end up putting the woman on trial trying to defend their client. Now for the important question many ask.

What should I do if I am being assaulted?

There are many theories and opinions on this. Here is a link to a good article on this topic at PBS.org. https://www.pbs.org/kued/nosafeplace/studyg/rape.html. Some studies show that fighting back decreases the risk, other differ. I will not give an opinion on this since I am not an expert in that field. The one thing that all studies agree upon is that the important thing to do is live through it. Most times this will be a judgment call depending on where the attack occurs. Meaning, is it near where people could hear you scream, are you in a desolate area, is it a home invasion, etc. There are home security systems that provide a button you can carry in your pocket or a chain around your neck. These are great when you are home because you can activate the panic alarm from anywhere in your house that will make noise, and your monitoring system will dispatch the police. The alarm sounding will cause most perpetrators to want to get out.

These are all things that you can research. Many vehicles are equipped with panic buttons if you are subscribed to the service plan that when activated, the dispatch center knows your exact GPS location and dispatched help. Where do you draw the line on your protection? Those are all personal choices. Think back to aware awareness and protection chapters. Anything you do is better than doing nothing. Awareness and protection is the key. About a taser or mace, I strongly suggest you speak to your local police department who will gladly advise you in the proper course of what is best for you. As we proceed into the next few chapters, you will read more true stories that reflect the topics we are discussing during that chapter.

CHAPTER 7

REPORT IT OR NOT?

As we discussed earlier, the two main reason why women do not report abuse is fear and embarrassment. Many women fear the need to testify in court or have their child testify in court. By the nature of television shows, they surmise what they could be facing. The sad part is, most of that is true. This part of the healing process can be most difficult since the woman is reliving every moment in detail. When this involves a child, the process is not public and much greater precautions are taken to assure the psychological well-being of the child. Let us look at the sixth amendment, (rev. 1992), courtesy of Google.com.

"In all criminal prosecutions, the accused shall enjoy the right to a speedy and public trial, by an impartial jury of the State and district wherein the crime shall have been committed, which district shall have been previously ascertained by law, and to be informed of the nature and cause of the accusation; to be confronted with the witnesses against him; to have compulsory process for obtaining witnesses in his favor, and to have the Assistance of Counsel for his defense.

It is self-explanatory. The part I want to point out is **"to be confronted with the witness against him."** Every person being accused of a crime has the right to be confronted by those accusing them. Which also gives their attorney the right to cross-examine that individual. Many times, we all hear the phrase, "This case will be tried by the public." What that means is, public opinion could sway a jury or possibly a judge. This is done by the statements attorneys may make that are picked up by the news media and made public. I will not give my opinion as to whether I believe that is true or not, and you can decide for yourself. However, I do believe that our justice system is not perfect, and certainly has room for improvement. Many laws that were passed at the time, for those times, are old and do not apply in today's society. However, with that said, I also believe that although not perfect, it is the best system on the planet. Nothing will ever be perfect, and always has room for improvement. The problem is a result of the time and red tape involved to institute change.

Sexual assault is not limited to domestic violence, or random acts to the public. These assaults occur in high schools and colleges. Although college campuses are highly protected by the school's security staff, no one can be in every place at the same time. College campuses are not gated facilities. Many do have guard locations at the entrances to parking lots. However, anyone could park their car somewhere and walk around campus. These people prey on the students that are walking alone at night. Many schools have volunteer students that will escort someone where they are going at night if they are alone. When I was in college, I served on one of those teams. However, the best practice of prevention is for a woman not to be walking alone around campus at night. Some campuses have shuttle buses that run for students to use. Each school is different. One of the things as a parent you may want to look into when your child is applying for college.

There are numerous reason why every physical or sexual assault should be reported. The main reason should be obvious. You want to stop the person from doing it again to someone else, or even you. Assailants have been known to victimize a person more than once. No one should ever be shamed into reporting a case of abuse. Some may think they should do whatever it takes to get a person to report abuse. However, during the process, which will be more than one conversation, someone can cause a much deeper emotional problem. They will be making the person feel as if they did something wrong, when in fact, they did not. That woman was the victim. Never forget that. These things should be discussed, as the woman feels ready to discuss them. To try to drag things out of them is completely counter-productive and damaging. People know right from wrong. Whether they are choosing not to report something, they still know the act was wrong. Keep in mind what we discussed that a woman will go through when she reports this. I am not saying you should not advise someone to report it, I am merely implying that you do NOT shame them into it, and help them through this difficult period. Many women do not have a support system that can help them get through these difficult times. Many articles have been written by various media as to why a woman would even want to report it. Here is a link to an article by the HuffPost updated on 8/12/2016. Since that article, many things have gotten better, especially with the workplace doing better training. However, the general population might still feel things like this still continue. https://www.huffingtonpost.com/entry/rape-victims-report-police_us_57ad48c2e4b071840410b8d6. Prison overcrowding continues to be a problem.

I hear this all the time, *"They should lock them up."* Okay, I agree. Where do you have in mind? Prisoners are getting early releases that committed lesser crimes to make room for others. We do not have enough prison facilitates. No one wants a prison in their town. In this writers opinion, the larger question is, what are we doing wrong that we need this many prisons? What are we missing? That is a simple question to answer. To have the correct size police force to decrease crime costs money. That money comes from taxes. Taxes that people already believe are high enough. We are faced with a double-edged sword, one that is getting sharper and cutting deeper each year. We live in a statistical world. There are data and stats for just about everything. Coming from the fire service and commercial ambulance service, everything is based on data. Times of the days where call volume is the highest, what areas of the city have the highest call volume and when. This goes down to the level of demographics. Age groups, nature of calls, type of injuries, etc. The reports that are run to track these things are based on KNOWN factors. From this data, police, fire, and EMS crews could staff and position themselves accordingly. When a crime is not reported, the data is no longer accurate. Therefore, the appropriate agency cannot target these problem areas. The hardest thing for anyone to do is stand up and speak out. Being at the end of the limb of a tree is a very lonely place, and often times, it is not a popular place to be.

Watch the news. How many times does one person speak out when they are sexually abused by someone of popularity, or running for a political office? Shortly after, others seem to appear and speak out. This is another reason to report it. Our society comes together as a group, much easier than speaking out alone. However, it takes one person to start that ball rolling. We need to face reality as well. There are cases when someone is an opportunist, and there are those that will join in to get a piece of the pie. Thankfully, those cases are rare. However, to discuss this topic intelligently, we MUST, or should I say, are OBLIGATED to look at all points. When these accusations are made, it starts an investigation to verify the validity of the claim. We can only hope that whatever the truth is, comes out. This type of abuse or accusations does not enjoy the benefits of forensic science. In 2015, 149 people were cleared for crimes they were convicted of due to forensic science, their claim of innocence was true, and they were released. I am sure that number is higher now. However, there still needs to be a system of checks and balances. It is impossible to know the exact number of physical abuse or rape cases that go unreported each year, simply because no one knows about them. Rainn.org has some interesting data on this. Certain types of assaults have decreased over time. Others have not. When you lump sexual violence into one category, the numbers look better. Now take those numbers and break them down into individual types of sexual violence and it paints a slightly different picture. The reason for these discrepancies is due to lack of reporting.

Writing something that I have seen written many times, *"because it's the right thing to do,"* insults your intelligence. Reporting is also a key to prevention. Many of these assailants will go on to do it again. Reporting it and them being caught, does not save you from your experience, but it can save someone else from experiencing the same. Reporting is a critical part of prevention. I can list many reasons why a woman does not report this type of crime.

- Shame,
- Made to feel as though it is their fault,
- The belief is that the system is not set up properly,

- Many never get arrested or serve time. Therefore, they are still out in society living their life while I suffer from the pain,
- A parent wants to protect their child,
- Embarrassment
- I just want to forget it.

The list goes on. At one meeting, a woman was telling her story. She was raped at school. When she reported it, she felt the school wanted to keep it quite not to draw bad publicity. She went directly to the police. Not to divulge the type of school or the area where she lived at the time, this occurred in a town that heavily relied on the revenue that was brought it. When she met with the detective, she stated he suggested why ruin someone's life. She stated he asked if there was something, she might have done to provoke this. After a few more questions along those lines, she left and withdrew her complaint. She was speaking out to bring this to the attention of others. Many articles on the internet refer to this same type of treatment. We must ask ourselves, why would a woman report it? Feeling as if their level of self-worth and self-respect has been diminished is bad enough without adding this to the mix. However, the truth is, if someone is treated in that manner, that also needs to be reported as well. *No one can fix a problem that no one complains about.* That does not make you the bad person; it makes you the smart one. Every story is a difficult one because someone had to endure that pain. Keep reading, because the most traumatic of stories, a story that made this subject so passionate for me, is still yet to come.

Reporting any crime is a painstaking experience, and yes, reporting a sexual assault crime is even more painstaking because so many emotions are involved. However, I cannot express how important it is to report these brutal crimes. With all things in life, it is your choice. It is a choice you must be comfortable with. It is a proven fact that when we face our issues, we can eventually get closure. We will never receive closure when it is lurking in the background. Do not believe that a sexual crime will be forgotten easily. It will not. However, the human brain has the unique ability in time to push things to the back that are traumatic experiences.

Look at your brain as a huge filing cabinet. The brain will try to keep the things of pleasure in the top draw, and things that are traumatic in the bottom drawer. That is the draw that in time, you rarely open. It is a process. With the proper help, guidance, and support, it can be a successful process. I know I am hammering this point, but it is an important one. Switching gears for a moment, we need to address a different age group, children.

*****

People are precious. However, our children are most dear to us. Child sexual abuse does not only affect females, but it is also very prevalent in males as well. Please note, 1in6.org states that researchers use "sexual abuse" to describe experiences in which children are subjected to unwanted sexual contact involving force, threats, or a large age difference between the child and the other person (which involves a big power differential and exploitation). As you can see, the description is wide and can involve a variety of issues. Researchers have found that 1 in 6 men have experienced some form of sexual abuse or assault, whether in childhood or as adults. This does not include noncontact experiences, which can also have a negative effect. These effects can be long-lasting. The statistics on this are concerning. For a full list, here is the link to invisible children 2017 statistics on invisiblechildren.org.

http://www.invisiblechildren.org/2017/12/29/child-abuse-statistics-the-best-resources/?gclid=Cj0KCQjw9NbdBRCwARIsAPLsnFYTt DKaW0C0vloWGH6a3iSz2Che7l1kc8nDSMe3K1IkfQqbrrlcdFcaA n2aEALw_wcB

These numbers represent reality. Much of what we never hear about. This site does not allow sharing. I cannot copy the data into this book. Child sexual abuse can happen anywhere. Over the recent years, finding out that these occurrences have happened in schools and churches has been at the least, shocking. However, many occur at home by siblings, parents, or other family members. Besides the pain that can be associated with child sexual abuse, emotional abuse is very serious. Depending on the age of the child, they do not understand what has happened or why. Many think it is because they did something wrong and are being punished. Reporting these cases is so important to the future emotional well-being of a child. I mentioned a case earlier where the parents moved. I do not agree with that. However, I can understand it. As much as things involving minors are supposed to be sealed, somehow, things get out, especially if it is a public criminal offense versus within a family. Most everything that is public makes the news. A parent wants to save their child from that embarrassment. Parents are very protective, but that protectiveness can make them blind at times. That does not mean they do not want the best for their child. They are so hurt all they want to do is shelter their child. Their intentions are well placed, but the methods may not be the best.

Every responder is a child advocate and a mandatory reporter. Meaning, we must report any suspicion of child abuse in any form to whatever the local child protective service agency is. Knowing what happens if I made a report; I had to be completely sure my suspensions were correct. When a child protective service gets involved, some things go into motion. Initially, if the police agree, they can take custody of the children or child. A complete and thorough investigation occurs. It is a life-altering experience for a family, but it is unavoidable if it helps one child. There are many signs we look for.

- Unexplainable bruises
- Bruises that do not match the story
- A child's fear of one or more parents
- The environment
- The way parents interact with first responders

These are all red flags we look for. When a child fears something, they shut down. Handling a child is completely different. On a positive note, when we will report something, the child receives the help they need and is protected. Once child services are involved, the parents have little say. Their concern is for the safety and the well-being of the child. Do mistakes happen? Yes, they do. Here is a story from a woman who had a bad experience. The police were called to her house because someone called complaining a baby would not stop crying. The mother had an infant. Her husband worked overnights, and she had two other children. The baby was having problems with the formula they were using and would become colicky. She tried to explain this to the officer when they arrived. The other two children awoke, and one had a few bruises that were at different stages of healing. They are evident by their color. She tried to explain he was always falling while playing in the yard.

We cannot blame the officer(s). Their intentions were probably good. However, they did not call EMS to evaluate the children. Child services were notified, and EMS was called to transport the children to the hospital. This turned into a major investigation. The family was interviewed, friends, schools, employers, the children's doctor, and a full home environment evaluation was done. I believe you could see how embarrassing something like this could be. The children were temporality taken for the home. If they did not have a family, they would have gone into foster care. However, in this case, they were placed with the grandparents. After weeks of investigation, everything checked out, and the children were returned. We need to ask ourselves a few questions.

1. Was this necessary?
2. What emotional impact did, or could it have?
3. What are the lingering effects?

First, I never play Monday morning quarterback. If the officer felt this was merited, then so be it. The children's safety is paramount. Would someone else handle it differently? Maybe, but we will never know. If I were on that call, I would have not reported anything until the children had a complete medical exam. In a world where liability is such a great concern, people do not want to take the chance of being sued. However, sometimes we need to look at the bigger picture. In this case, the big picture was to get the children out of the house. That could have been done without a child services report unless the mother refused to have them checked, which she claimed she was never asked, and would not have refused. Once the children were checked, the hospital could have made the report if they felt it necessary.

Do we jump the gun sometimes? In this case, the family suffered extreme emotional distress from this, as did the children. It now raised questions about the parents with friends, family, and employers. The children were traumatized because they were separated from their parents. This family survived, this woman was there to help others who may have experienced the same thing. The effects of this event can linger for some time. Will people look at them the same? In this case, they did not. Her husband eventually lost his job. For somethings, being safe than sorry is a good approached. At times, not so much. In defense of the officer, sometimes this can be a very grey area and a thin line. I am sure they did what they thought was best. This family struggled and survived. You can decide for yourself if all this was necessary. These are just some of the things that people do not consider. Things the news does not tell you, and true stories from those who have experienced it. I said this earlier. Data and statistics are fine to get an idea of the scope of a problem, the truth lies with those who have experienced it. These are the stories that no one ever hears.

In most cases, no one hears about child sexual abuse or female abuse until it hits the news, it happens to them, or someone they know. In most cases even then, they would say, *"That will never happen to me,"* or, *"I'm glad that wasn't me."* To reality is, it can happen to anyone at any time.

In closing this chapter, the key take-home message is these attacks should be reported. As difficult as it may be, the only way to stop someone from doing this to someone else is to report it. The system will not change overnight. It will have its flaws. That is where our lawmakers must step in. Do we live in a Band-Aid system, where it fixes it for now and does not consider the future? I would say yes in many cases. Lawmakers want to attack what the voters are concerned about this very instant. They will remember that when elections come. However, this never solves a problem for the long term. What are the deterrents? Do most of these people getting off, or getting away with it become a deterrent? Of course not, and it never will be. As difficult as this might be to say, to control crime better, the punishment must be severe if convicted. For some crimes, there should be no plea-bargaining. Of course, these are all opinions, and everyone is entitled to their own. However, these are many of the reason people do not report these brutal and violent crimes.

CHAPTER 8

WHEN LIFE GETS DIFFICULT

Does Life get difficult? You bet it does. Different events result in different aftermath. In the case of domestic violence, it is a daily fear. A woman never knows what will trigger an event, and lives a life of constant fear, especially when there are children in the house. The same applies to domestic violence cases when substance abuse such as drugs or alcohol are concerned. I have been told stories from women that were out in public at a wedding or another event with their partner who was starting to drink heavily. Knowing what happens when they drink too much, they would make a simple request for them to slow down, which would cause a scene in public. This could be very embarrassing at a family function or restaurant.

In many cases, this would result in domestic violence when they got home later. In cases of domestic violence, a woman never knows what might trigger an outburst. They are most comfortable when their partner is at work, or not home. When they returned home, they would walk around guarded, always being agreeable, and not saying anything. Their anxiety and fear level increased exponentially. Can you imagine living day in and day out like that? Maybe you are living that way now. When I worked as a professional firefighter/paramedic and part-time for a commercial ambulance service, I worked an average of 70 plus hours a week. I responded to an average of 48 to 52 medical calls per week, caring for 76,251 patients during my years on the road. I would respond to an average of 15 domestic violence calls per week, mostly in the evening hours. In our region, I was one of 381 paramedics. Assuming I was not the only paramedic that responded to domestic violence calls, do the math. The numbers are frightful. Many of the calls were multiple visits to the same address.

In almost 80% of these cases, the one that caused the disturbance was intoxicated. In almost all of the cases, the woman did not want to press charges. In many of these repeated calls, with help, things can get better. In most cases, they do not, mostly because the offending party refuses to get help. Sometimes it takes an arrest to turn the light on in someone's head. The police are in a difficult position when it comes to domestic violence. Most calls come in from outside parties complaining about the yelling or noise, especially late in the evening. If the woman denies any physical violence, which may or may not be true, the police try to defuse the situation. Many times, they will state that if they have to come back, they will make an arrest. Domestic violence charges are of a nature that no one wants to have on their record, therefore, for that event, that usually solves the issue, until the next time. This can go on multiple times, over time, until it will eventually become physical. Alcohol or drugs are mind-altering agents. Once someone losses control while under the influence, anything is possible. I had seen children struck by a father when they tried to help their mother who was being hit. When there are clear signs of violence, an arrest will be made. In those cases, the victim does not have to press charges, and it is worked out in the court system. The sad part is, we have to ask, why a woman tolerates this behavior. Those reasons we discussed earlier.

This makes day-to-day life very difficult. Many times, I have responded to schools to evaluate a child due to a teacher finds welts or bruises on them. There are times a woman is physically attacked because she is trying to stop her partner from striking their child. So puts herself in the middle. Sometimes this works, other times, she takes a beating, and the child still is hit. Some may think poorly of these women. Do not. If you have never been in a situation where things seem hopeless, and you feel trapped, you cannot understand what is going on in their minds. Once depression, low esteem, and loss of self-respect set it, no one is thinking logically. This is why as medical personnel, are training to be objective and not subjective is so strong. A paramedic in training will care for well over 500 patients before they ride with a doctor and are cleared to function on their own. They made INSTANT life and death decisions. You could go from pronouncing a baby dead from SIDs in their crib to taking care of an elderly patient with a swollen angle and have to bury those emotions. In my career, I have pronounced over 2,000 patients deceased, across all ages. The youngest being four years ago, and had to testify at the murder trial. Life does not become difficult for only one person. It becomes difficult for many. Picture this in your mind for a moment.

You are the medical person who just responded to a suspected child rape call. When you arrive, the evidence is very clear that a parent, who is intoxicated, did this to this child. The rage you feel inside, especially if you have children, is tremendous. Your urge to strike out MUST be controlled. Your immediate concern is for the child. Do you think life will be difficult for this family? You bet it will. After any traumatic event, the death of a family member, a pet, loss of employment, and more, life always gets more difficult. However, it is usually more short term. The effects of female abuse in any form or child abuse in any form, the effects are more long term. It takes a great deal of time to get through these issues. The effects as I mentioned earlier, are systemic. They do not only involve one person, but they could also involve many. The degree of involvement or effect is different for each individual involved. Although I only speak at two or three of these meetings a year when invited, I have seen women who have healed and overcome their experience. They continue to come to help others. I have also seen the same woman there for months that have still not reached that point of healing.

During this time, and for a long time after, life is different. It will be. This is not a fall and scrap to the knee. This is one of the most personal violations imaginable. Let us look at some of the issues that people face during the aftermath:

- Emotional detachment to their partner,
- Anxiety, depression,
- Introverted behavior,
- Finances,
- Family stress,
- Nightmares,
- Lack of sleep and appetite,
- Lack of motivation,
- Low self-esteem,
- Low self-respect
- Feelings of being judged or labeled by others.

These are only a few. These women feel so violated many times their emotional and intimate relationship with their partner are gone. This is not by choice; it is a result of reliving the event in their mind. Physical contact is a reminder of the event. After some time, this also wears on the partner.

In many cases, these women cannot even tolerate a hug or a kiss, allowing no contact at all. This leads to anxiety, depression, and stress. It puts additional tension in the relationship. The women will become introverted, meaning, she will turn inside herself. She will become quiet, non-social, and not wanting to talk. Her self-esteem and self-respect are very low, wondering if her partner will even want her anymore. Sleeping becomes difficult due to nightmares; therefore, they do not want to sleep. This state of clinical depression also causes them to have reduced appetite resulting in weight loss, lack of energy, and motivation. If there are young children in the household, they are too young to understand, which puts additional responsibilities on their partner, which in time causes additional issues for them. They do not want to socialize, or even go out in public for fear of being judged by others, or "labeled as the woman who was raped." People do not inherently mean to be cruel, but curiosity is part of the human condition. Finances soon become an issue. If her partner normally works overtime, that may have to change due to their additional responsibilities to this situation. If the woman works, she may use all her vacation and/ or sick time. If she is not ready to return to work, there could be a loss of income. Many employers offer short-term disability to their employees, but many do not.

Anything that effects finances is always a problem. The banks and credit cards do not care. The utilities do not care. Everyone wants to be paid. All the "I'm sorry to hear of your misfortune," does not pay the bills. There is no light shining at the end of the tunnel. There is no way of knowing when the light will start to shine. This is the reason why professional help is so important. It is amazing how we take the simplest of tasks granted. They become so difficult when we cannot do them. How no doubt, these are life-changing and altering experiences. I have also had the sad experience to respond to calls for women who have attempted suicide after a violent physical assault. I dislike using the word rape. It is a terrible word, although accurate to describe the event. The form of physical violence is much different from a physical assault due to a domestic violence argument. Even a case of rape during a domestic dispute, which also happens, is not as traumatic as when acted upon by a stranger. People ask, *"How could a husband be considered as raping their wife."* Keep in mind, rape is a violent, brutal, criminal act performed against an unwilling party. Two people being married does not change the definition.

A woman was telling her story when she caught her husband cheating on her with a younger woman. He ended the affair because he did not want a divorce and admitted he was wrong. However, his wife refused to be intimate with him. That is a normal response. I will not judge how long that response should continue. Each circumstance is different, and each person will react differently. Most men realize they will pay for their wrong actions. The question is, how long? How long should they have to pay? Should a woman reach a point where she realizes she cannot forgive and forget, cannot move forward, and simply should decide to end the relationship? To continue the story, she refused to have intimate relations with her husband for about six months. One night he came how and had too much to drink. When he attempted to be intimate with her, she refused. He proceeded to force himself upon her having intercourse. Yes, this is rape. She was not a willing participant. He was arrested, which eventually they repaired the damage, and the charges were dropped. After counseling, they were working this out, and things were getting better between them. What I learned for her story was, the emotional impact, although great, was different. Since this was her husband and not a stranger, her outlook on the event was different. This is not to say that every woman would react that way, it just shows that circumstances and the people involved could have an effect on the impact to a woman. I could not find any studies that were done related to this specific type of abuse.

Nothing is life is written in stone. At this point, we have been discussing woman from what I refer to as the general population, what most would consider a generally accepted lifestyle. Earlier I mentioned environments could be a factor. To explore that, I need to be more specific. There are different cultures and environments in our worlds. In some cultures, whether you agree with this or not, a man intimating takes a woman whenever he wants. The woman expects this. Even if she is unwilling, it is an accepted practice in that culture. Therefore, the woman may not look at this as a form of rape, even though she was unwilling. Since this is an objective, not a subjective topic, I will not refer to any specific culture. It is not my intent to pass judgment on cultural beliefs. This just speaks to the differences. Also, some women are involved in certain activities where having sex with many different men, even if they do not want to, is part of that culture of the environment. Is that rape? The legal definition of rape in the United States is as follows.

Rape *in the United States is **defined** by the Department of Justice as "Penetration, no matter how slight, of the vagina or anus with any body part or object, or oral penetration by a sex organ of another person, without the consent of the victim."*

In the last two examples, the women involved may have been unwilling, but allowed to act to occur. Does that fit the definition? Could there be a grey area? This is one of the reasons that it may be sometimes difficult to get a conviction because it lends a defense attorney to use many avenues to present a defense.

Therefore, most woman will take the stand that so as not to get hurt further, they let it happen, rather than fight the assailant and risk being beaten. Could this be an example of a law that needs more definition?

Now comes the part you may not like. Here is a scenario I came across during my career. I am sure you have heard of many such cases on the news. A girl is at a party, drinks too much and has sex with someone, which is something she knows she would never normally do, wake up the next day, remembers the event, and claims she was raped. There are cases on the internet that resemble this exact situation. The girl had no bruises or marks on her body to indicate she put up a struggle. Witnesses said they saw her go into a bedroom with the student she accused of raping her. What happened behind closed doors? What do you think her chance is of winning this case? I do not know the outcome of the accusation. Could these be the types of cases that are never be reported due to embarrassment, or not wanting their parents to find out? Whichever it is, they also come with life changes after the event. Therefore, you can see there is a broad spectrum to this topic. There are two factors when it comes to young adults. Let's face it, we were all young adults at one point, so no one takes offense.

1. They think they know it all,
2. They are not mature enough in all areas of life to make the correct choices

This is NOT knocking our young adults. It is simply a fact. So many kids go off to college not being able to do their own laundry, or balance their checkbook, how can we expect them to make the right sexual choices? We live in a world where sex is more widely accepted and open. To our young people, it is innocent and fun. However, when it is not innocent or fun, it has devastating effects because they have not reached that level of maturity. Sexual inferences are used to promote products in TV commercials, make movies and TV series more interesting, and many books are written with sexual content in it. There is no book rating system. Anyone could buy it. How does a writer write a love story without a sex scene? There is an answer to that question. I even made a blog post about how to write a classy love scene. We must ask ourselves, is the love scene that is the issue, or is it the way it is written? I am NOT pointing the finger at anyone or placing blame anywhere. This is what our society has evolved to, and appears to feel is acceptable. I have my opinions on these matters, which I will not state. This is not a subjective book of my opinions. It is a book of facts. People need to establish their own opinions. Every one degree of what is acceptable is different, which is based on what they enjoy. I have responded to houses for a medical call that when I walk in, there is an adult channel playing on the television with young children in the same room. There, I draw the line.

The biggest problem lies in the fact that people in general, do not think before they act. What example was set for those children? What can we expect, as they get older? What will they think is acceptable and not acceptable behavior? What of the child that consistently sees their father or mother fondle each other in their presence as they are growing? Will they think that behavior is acceptable and take that with them into their relationships? Could this be the starting point where life gets difficult? These are all good questions. Child Development has published studies regarding the effects of what a child experiences that affect their adult life. As you can see, life can get very difficult for a wide variety of reasons, and the topic of female abuse goes much deeper than what appears on the surface. How many movies have you gone to with adult content, or violence, where parents have brought children that in your opinion are too young to be seeing these types of movies? What children see, they will take as being what is normal. Why wouldn't they? Therefore, a child that is raised in a household where domestic violence occurs will grow up to feel it is normal, as they may take on that behavior, or they will never want it to be a part of their life. CDV.org has some startling data on this. Here are a few key points to know. I recommend you use this link to see a full study. https://cdv. org/2014/02/10-startling-domestic-violence-statistics-for-children/.

- Children who are raised in a domestic violence household are three times more likely to repeat the cycle in their adult years

- In a household with domestic violence, you are 74% more likely to commit a violent crime against another
- Children in these households display the effect of post-traumatic stress disorder (PTSD)
- Children from homes with domestic violence have a more difficult time learning in school
- Those children are also 50% **more likely** to use drugs or alcohol and commit suicide.

These are some of the more pertinent facts, there are many more in the link I provided you. There are many more studies, but the numbers do not vary much. Life starts getting difficult for many reasons at a very young age. I wanted to spend some time discussing children. People do not realize how widespread abuse is. Especially the effects it has, and where this could begin. This information is important to know fully understand this topic. When life gets difficult, everything and every aspect of life becomes difficult. Simple tasks are no longer simple tasks, logic, and rational thinking changes. The ability to understand things is clouded by emotions. A staircase that spirals downward rapidly, to the point that pulling out of that spin can be impossible. People who were never mediated for emotional disorders may now need to be for the rest of their life. They can lose a sense of who and what they are. Their behavior can become erratic and unpredictable. These are the things that can happen during the aftermath when life changes. Prevention, awareness, and if it occurs, help is the answer to avoid these things from happening to you.

CHAPTER 9

CAN YOU SURVIVE IT?

Yes, you can survive it. If you are strong enough, you can survive anything. The key is to form a plan and stick with it. That plan should always start with getting help. The first time I was invited to speak at a woman's support group, I was amazed at the number of women that attended, and the variety of issues that were discussed. I was impressed by the atmosphere that was created. The group counselor created a comfortable, non-judgmental; speak when you are ready to speak environment. The group leader was outstanding. Imagine how I felt the first time. Honestly, I was nervous as hell, which is not normal for me. I was well prepared, and well versed on the topic, but to see the faces of the women made me wonder, *what in the hell can I possibly say to them?* To my surprise, it could not have gone any better. Share stories and experiences were paramount. I believe that is what gained me their trust. I went dressed very relaxed, which I normally do. Unless I am hired for a company seminar, or to speak at a college as a guest lecture, when I meet with book clubs or other groups, I want them to feel relaxed. I do not like to present myself as thinking I am better than they are. First, I do not believe that. If any speaker puts up that wall, they will not be able to tear it down. I sat on a table, introduced myself. I did not want to try to impress them with my credentials. I started by asking, who would like to ask me a question? From there, it could not have gone any better, and I was invited back. I NEVER charge a fee for these types of visits to groups, book clubs, high schools, or any community event. This is not about money. It is all about helping people if I can, even if it is to provide them with an alternative way of looking at things.

Surviving anything has a great deal to do with your support system. Your support system could be all, or a combination of family, friends, and co-workers. Everyone has heard the term *"support system."* However, most do not know what that actually means. They only know what they think it means. Let us look at what it DOES NOT mean.

- It does not mean that people judge you,
- It does not mean that people give you their opinion,
- It does not mean that people tell you what to do,
- It does not mean that people tell you how to do it,
- It does not mean that people give you advice.

What it does mean is this.

- A support system is a network or group of individuals, or individual, that provide an individual practical or emotional support to a person.

That is it, plain and simple. Sometimes it just means giving someone a hug, holding a person's hand, or just listening. Making A person know you understand. It means you will OBJECTIVELY talk with them. No one person can effectively compare a situation they encountered to yours. The reason being as I stated earlier, each person is affected differently, and frankly, at the time, that person does not care what you experienced. All they are thinking about is what they went through. When I was instructing new paramedics, the one thing I taught them is, not every call you do will revolve around a life and death situation. Many times the best care you can give someone is to simply hold their hand, and comfort them to reduce their fears. Reducing a person's level of anxiety does many things. It lowers their heart rate, which lowers their blood pressure; it slows down their breathing and reduces their anxiety. Patients will take your lead. When they see you panic, they will panic. It stops their mind from getting on the anxiety merry-go-round. It also prepares them for what they are about to encounter when they get to a hospital. I call it emotional comforting.

In a sense, it is their support system at the time. A support system is not only about the victim, but it could also involve their family. Although a paramedic's initial responsibilities are to the patient, they are also for the family. If I responded to a cardiac arrest and started to work the patient, meaning trying to revive them, if I did not already know when I saw them, I would know in a matter of minutes if we were going to be successful, which is based on some factors. Once I determined this patient would not survive, while continuing our efforts, I would start to prepare the family for what I knew I was going to have to tell them. Make them part of the decision making process. Does it make the loss of a loved one easier, of course not? What it does is provide emotional support. They knew everything that could be done was, and make the ultimate end decision acceptable, thus, reducing the shock. These are all forms of support. If you are not the type of person that could do this, frankly, you are better off not being part of the process. You can do far more harm than good. Keep in mind you are dealing with someone who has recently experienced what is probably the most traumatic experience of their life. Even greater than losing a loved one? As much as losing a loved one is personal and painful, this type of abuse was a direct personal and physical attack. The effects are completely different.

Creating a positive atmosphere is also important. I am not saying have a celebration cake with balloons and noisemakers, I am referring to a positive attitude. Phrases like, *"I know how difficult this is for you,"* does not help. You do not; you did not go through it. You cannot know. The person suffering knows that, so why go there. Phrases such as, *"I know you are strong and can get through this, or we are all here to help you and are by your side,"* are all comforting and caring statements, and do not take anything away from the severity of the event. Never push people to talk. They will talk when they are ready. All you need to do is be there when that time comes, and LISTEN. Things such as, *"If you only took a different way home, or, if you didn't go to that party,"* and the worst of all, *"If you didn't piss him off."* All of those phrases suggest blame. Maybe they did something wrong. That is totally a negative approach as causes more harm than good. Being a good support person is not as easy as you think. Just due to the human condition, and human nature, everyone wants to state their opinion. This is NOT the time for your opinion. Many times I have been asked at a meeting, *"Did I do something wrong,"* or *"Should I have done something different?"* My reply is always, *"You did nothing wrong. You are not to blame. Understand that this type of behavior was not under your control, and is not acceptable under any circumstances."* This reinforces emotional support and reinforces that fact that they do not have any blame. That is positive reinforcement.

Let me add, that the examples I am using are my way of doing things, they are not intended as advice, or teaching you what to do or say. They are simply examples of negative and positive reinforcement. Everyone should do what works for them. How many times in your life were you talking to a friend about an issue, and they said, *"I felt good about until I talked to ....."* That is what you do not want. With children, it is even more delicate because when a child is scared, they shut down and do not say much. This takes a great deal of time and patience. A technique that is often used is a distracted conversation. Talk about something else. Something they enjoy and will talk about, and slowly and occasionally hit on the topic you wish to get them to discuss. Often times this is achieved by using their scenario as if it happened to someone else, and ask them their opinion. Whenever you are speaking to a child, remember. They are little people is size. To them, you appear as a giant and could frighten them. Be sure you are at their eye level, so they do not feel intimidated by your size.

Things such as hand gestures, facial expression, and body language can hint to what you are thinking. You do not have to say the words, because your body language just gave what you are thinking away. You must be calm, showing no outward signs that could be misread. Think about it. How many times have you asked someone a question to see how they respond? You use their words, as well as their body language to determine if what they are saying is true, genuine, or false. Anyone who does interviews, such as law enforcement personnel are trained in body language. If you cannot do this, never play poker for money. You will go broke. What makes a good poker player is the art of the "BLUFF." Their ability to control their appearance, rather than the hand they have. When you get anxious, the person you are trying to help will also get anxious. When you show signs of being nervous, they will get nervous. For most, this is very difficult to do, because people are naturally expressive. It is not a learned behavior, it is an innate behavior, meaning, we are born that way.

Now, all this time you thought supporting someone meant being a good friend. It is far more than that. This does not apply to every situation. If your girlfriend's boyfriend broke up with her in a text message, you might want to bash him. That is fine. I would like to as well. What we are referring here is more serious and important situations and forms of being part of a support system. I was asked once, *"My friend just wanted to sick there and get drunk while she talked. Should I let her?"* I will never advocate that you let someone sit and drink themselves drunk while they talk. Those choices are yours. If you do, be prepared to take responsibility for that person, which could mean driving them home, or spending the night with them to be sure they don't try and drive or do anything that may cause harm to them. Oh yes, many times I responded to calls of someone not breathing to find out they were drunk, vomited in their sleep and obstructive their airway causing them not to be able to breathe. If not corrected quickly, they will die. You are never helpful when you condone or allow someone to do anything that can cause them harm. In fact, in some cases, you might be held legally responsible if something does happen to them.

Does it seem like helping someone to survive an event is easy? Actually, it is; because you care. I realize this chapter makes it sound like a major project. It is just presenting alternative ways and things for you to consider in more severe circumstance. In one respect, for this particular subject, this chapter is also about awareness in a different form. I am not trying to scare you. However, with the right support and help, women can survive abuse and go on to have a normal and healthy life. Isn't that the end goal? We can never change what has happened, but we can change what could happen next. That is our goal. Keep another thing in mind. When you leave, you feel bad for what that are experiencing, but you are not the one living with it. You are not the one who has to face that person who hits them or gets back out into the world after a physical, sexual assault. You go back to your normal life, job, children, and family. They are still living with it. When they are alone is the worst time, the time their mind can wander. They will feel alone, and afraid.

Survival has many aspects. The two most important are the physical and emotional trauma, but it is not limited to physical injuries or emotional injuries. It has social implications as well as threatening all that you believe in. Your faith, your moral and value system, and makes a woman ask the most important question. WHY, WHY DID THIS HAPPEN TO ME?

YOU DID NOTHING WRONG

That is correct, you did nothing wrong. The fact is, there may never be a definitive answer to your question. There may be the case if the assailant is captured, they can provide an answer. Honestly, you may not want to hear the answer because no matter what it is, it will not make sense to you. How can any man be sick enough to physically beat or rape a woman is a question that has many answers. It could be Pandora's Box. One you may not want to open because one question and answer can lead to many more.

- If they are mentally disturbed, will that be enough for you to know?
- You will now want to know why he was out in public.
- Where did the system fail?
- Is he a repeat offender?
- If was in prison did he get out early and why?

Some women may find it hard to move on. Without an answer as to why, they do not feel as though they have closure. However, you can see that an answer opens the box to many more questions. The most difficult part of life is when we have to accept something without knowing why. Unbelievably, that is not a new concept. You deal with it at work every day. You are constantly tasked to do things without knowing why. All you ever know for sure, it has something to do you the company making more money. You do not question it. You do the task. It is not personal to you, so you do not care. However, this case is different. It is personal to you. You want to know. The human brain always searches for a reason because that is the human condition. You feel is you know why you might be able to accept it. That is an illusion you place in your mind to justify what you are feeling. It is similar to when someone passes away, and people ask God why he has taken them away. The spiritual answer is; God had another plan for them. That gives people comfort. That is a belief, not a fact. Yet, that belief provides comfort. In the case of domestic violence or physical, sexual assault, no belief can give you comfort. No spiritual terminology will give you comfort. Phrases such as, *"God works in mysterious ways,* or *God does not give you something you can't handle,"* do not seem to give you the comfort and answers you are looking for. At times, we need to accept that we may not know the answers.

Having closure is an interesting concept. I was married once to a woman that cheated on me. That is against every belief I have. Like most, I was quite hurt. I felt to have closure; I kept asking myself why and needed the answer. One day I realized something, and from that day on, the why was never important anymore. What I came to realize was, why will never change what happened. The best closure I could get is to accept what happened and move forward. I realize the comparison of events is not even close. However, this is about the concept, not the event. I have asked many women who have asked that question, "Why is having an answer so important?" If you know it, will you understand it and forgive?" I have NEVER gotten a yes answer, and I never will. Therefore, accept what has happened and work towards healing, getting back to your life and family, and look to your future. This is called positive reinforcement. To enable people to dwell on the things that may never know the answers to is anti-productive to their healing process. I am not a doctor. I have had extensive training on this topic, and as an education major, I was required to take psychology courses and went on to take more on my own. I love the field, but this stuff is common sense. People only need to get past "The Human Condition," and what is considered, "Human Nature," to see the sense in it.

Every woman I meet at a meeting or had the honor and privilege to care for is a survivor. No matter how traumatic the event, your heart is beating, you are breathing, and you survived. You survived what will probably be the most devastating experience in your life. Many women do not. Whether by suicide or being killed in the process, they did not survive. That itself is a tragedy. However, you are here. If you are a victim and reading this book, YOU ARE A SURVIVOR. Make that work for you, not against you. I always tell people not to look at what has happened. You cannot change that. Rather, look at what you have to live for. Survival is about strength, desire, and a willingness to overcome. It is about support, love, and determination. This is another reason

I was amazed at the survivors of these traumatic events. They have healed and moved on. They attend these meetings to help others. Somewhat in a way that cancer survivors help those that have diagnosed with the disease. As compared to society as a whole, they are a small, tight-knit group of women that understand. They get it. They have been there. They are heroes.

I met a woman who was sexually assaulted. She went through a very long period of depression and had more than one attempt at committing suicide. She was committed to programs on more than one occasion. She started heavily drinking and doing drugs. Eventually, her husband divorced her. He was granted full custody of their children. This did not make her healing process easier. In fact, it got worse. After many months of not seeing her children, and going on and out of the hospital and programs, she decided this was enough. She struggled very hard for a long time. She cleaned up her act before she even tried to contact her ex-husband. She had a job, her own apartment, attended this particular group and developed a strong support system. One day she reached out to her husband. He was happy to hear she was doing well. She wanted to start seeing her children. At first, he was hesitant and agreed only if he was present. This part of the healing process began. In time, she was able to see them more often, and they started doing things as a family, a picnic, dinner, or a movie. The outcome of her story is simple. In time, they all became very close again. She and her husband started working on their relationship. In my opinion, he never fell out of love with her, he probably did what he thought was best for his children. Eventually, they remarried, and she had that had a great life now. I could not help but feel a tear roll down my face. Sometimes people have to hit rock bottom, lose it all before that realize what is important. Many do, and many do not. She is probably one of the most courageous women I have ever met. As of the time of this writing, I have not been to that group in about six or seven months. However, I am willing to bet that if I were invited back, I would see her there helping others.

CHAPTER 10

WHAT WE SEE

This chapter can upset some. Remember, we MUST be objective, NOT subjective. Before we start, let me state that I am not giving you my opinion, I am stating simple facts. I did not include this under the chapter of why we should report it, because it is a subject matter of its own. However, it is related. WHAT WE SEE AND HEAR IN THE NEWS. This is nothing new. From the early days of the last presidential campaign, before it, and now, many women have come forward making many accusations of sexual assault or abuse against individuals running for office, or being considered for an appointment. I AM IN NO WAY IMPLYING THESE ARE NOT TRUE. The reality is, when an accusation speaks to an event that is 10, 20, 30 years, or older, there will automatically be doubt. The first questions raised will ALWAYS be why didn't you say something back then?

In many cases, the reason may be that times were different then. Women were not as outspoken about these things as they are now. Also, some women have stated that now the individual is a public figure, it is important for the American people to be aware of their past. These are all valid reasons. The problem sits with the credibility of the story. Many of these are so old that most people interviewed will not remember. This makes investigating these very difficult. This can cause someone that is guilty of the accusation to be exonerated. In all fairness, it could also be it is not true. Any man or woman that is an opportunist, is an extremely low percentage as compared to the rest of the population. In our justice system, we must look at all possibilities.

I was in the entertainment field many years ago. It was a known fact that sexual favors were exchanged for a variety of reasons for someone to get ahead. Get their shot as it is called. Does it make it right? ABSOLUTELY NOT. However, if it was consensual at the time, a person cannot come back years later and claim sexual assault or abuse. With that said, if the consensual encounter turned violent, that becomes a different case and should have been reported. The same holds true for some that exchange a sexual favor for compensation. Does this practice of sexual favors for money make someone a good man? I do not think. However, it was consensual sex. Maybe the people involved should have used better judgment. I understand that many years back women did not have the same opportunities for advancement that they have today, but is that really an excuse for that behavior? I know many women who have had these offers made to them and flatly refused them. It took them longer, but they succeeded. This topic is completely different than a brutally violent crime such as rape or domestic violence. In one sense, it sits in a category all of its own, which is why I am discussing it. Consensual means, both parties agreed to the act. It becomes a public-order crime when the act itself, consensual or not, is unlawful. A good example of that would be prostitution in a state where it is illegal. It is a consensual act, but the manner in which the act occurred, meaning for monetary gain, is illegal.

In society today, this issue is gaining more news coverage, and more issues of this nature surface each day. Also, it trickles down to other areas that are much less severe. Let me give you an example of a real case. Here is the scenario.

A woman was walking into a bar. She walked by three men having a conversation while sitting at the bar with the bartender. Some off-color remarks were made as the four men were laughing and talking. These remarks were NOT about the woman. What she heard she found offensive and complained to the owner, which resulted in the bartender being fired.

Should he have been terminated? Think about that before you decide. Why is this example important? In any society, anything can be taken too far. I am sure by now you have formed your opinion as to whether his termination was justified. Here are the results of the case. The bartender sued the owner. He won the case. He won the case on the merits of free speech, and if the woman found the conversation offensive, she could have taken a different path away from the conversation, or left the bar.

So what is the moral of this example? We live in a constant state of existence, which is called life. In life, things will happen. Many times, these are not intentional, and every person has the right to walk away from it. No one can constantly be looking in every direction, and thinking of every word they say before they say it for fear of offending someone. Now, if the situation were such where the woman was sitting at the bar, they knew she was there, or the comment was made about her, that becomes a different situation. How many times in your life, whether you are a man or a woman have you said something, noticed someone heard and apologized? My next question to you is, do you think all this media coverage of these events causes a false statement to be made about people just for the publicity? Let me repeat. I am not saying this occurs, I am merely bringing out various possibilities since this is such a prominent issue on the news every day. I also think back before our recent presidential campaign. Before that campaign and issues were raised during that campaign, these things rarely if ever where heard about on the news. Since that time, they are now weekly events.

To be frank, anyone who runs for public office will always be under the microscope. They pay that price. If they do not like it, pick a different profession. There is more scandal when you read articles about movie stars and sports players than anything else. However, that is accepted. It is looked upon as gossip. Do we live in a selective world, where only some are judged for an action when that same action is fine for others? Except for a governor or higher elected officials; sports players, movie stars, and music performers are idolized and admired far more than any elected official is. This applies to all age groups. Yet, we accept that behavior from them. Is society partially to blame? Can we hang someone out to dry, when we support others that do the exact same thing? Is that fair and equal justice? If our president took a knee during the paying of the national anthem, people would look to impeach him, but when a sports player does it, it is freedom of expression. Yes, it upsets many, but they are still collecting on their multi-million dollar contracts. Standards or acceptable standards must apply to everyone equally to have an equal and balanced society. In a perfect world that is true, however, we do not live in a perfect world. How does all of this apply to *A Woman's Fear?* It applies because a woman realizes the system is not perfect, which increases their fear to report abuse resulting in an increased fear of it occurring.

What other things do not help women? Frankly, some of the things some woman do when they protest. I cannot count the number of bleeps I have heard on the news from things some woman yell out during a protest. That may be their right, but it does not help their cause. To be perceived as being credible and taken seriously, any person must present himself or herself that way. This is so important because it directs public perception and public opinion. This is one of the main reasons in this book I do not state my opinions. I state the facts and give you things to think about. My opinion on many topics in this book is not important, but the facts are. The one opinion I have that is important is that female abuse is not acceptable. To be clear, let me define abuse. ***Abuse is something that is used to create a bad effect, or for a bad purpose. It is intentional. Treat a person or animal with cruelty or violence, especially regularly or repeatedly.*** Anything consensual, accidental, or with no malleus intended, does not fall under that definition. Therefore, I can comfortably state my opinion that I am against female abuse in any form and support every woman, or a woman's group that feels the same way.

We see much of this in everyday life. Put any group of men together, or any group of woman together, and things that could offend someone can be said. I have said that woman are much more outspoken in today's society. That does not only refer to coming forward to raise awareness. That refers to everything; their thoughts, the way they speak, as well as act. Women are much more independent or were they always independent, but now it is more widely accepted? With any form of independence, comes responsibility. An independent man or woman will be judged differently because they are more outspoken. Look at like that one bad apple in a bushel. One bad apple does not spoil the whole bunch. However, most will pass over that bushel and reach into the next. Society will tend to judge an entire gender based on what one or more people of gender do. Ladies, how many women do you know that have the opinion that ALL MEN SUCK? Clearly of the result of someone that hurt someone along the way. Maybe it happened by more than one man? I am a man, and I do not suck? I prefer NOT to be lumped into a group with others. My ex-wife cheated on me, I do not say all women suck. Being independent in your thinking is one thing, generalizing is another. This is the reason why some groups, male and female, get a bad rap. Any human rights groups should be about preaching their beliefs, NOT bashing a complete gender, regardless of who is doing it. You may think this is off topic, but that is far from the truth.

Under every major issue, are underlying issues. Some which may have contributed to a particular problem. Unless you know of them and understand them, you will never totally understand the main issue. Sometimes it is not about where we are at, it is about how we got there. Often times to fix that decreases the larger issue. One of the other issues is we are always living in a three-generational world. Meaning, there are three main generations of people. Keep in mind that each generation has their opinions that will never match, based on the upbringing and experience, which was different for each generation. This creates a plethora of different ideas and opinions. This will always cause a clash between the generations. Degrees of acceptance will greatly vary between them. A performer on stage that makes a remark about what they may do if something occurs will be supported by our youth frowned upon by their parents and despised by the elderly, three different generations resulting in three different viewpoints. That will apply to almost every subject matter in the world ranging from war to peace. These opinions will have a great impact on what happens when it comes to what people, and what generation people will cater too.

There is one more thing I want to discuss in this chapter before we move on that I feel is pertinent to the main topic. That is perception. The unique thing about perception is how you perceive something, is different from how others may perceive it. Especially when communicating. You may know what you are trying to say, but others may not perceive it the same way. Let us look at TV commercials for a moment or TV shows. Commercials reflecting certain products are more sexually orientated than for other products. Thinking back when I was growing up, a woman was never portrayed in a bra and panties in a commercial for women's underwear. Look at that for a moment. Are they really that much difference between advertising and showing a woman in a bathing suit? However, the fact that it is for underwear makes it perceived differently. If a woman went to the beach in her bikini, or string bikini, that would be accepted. Let her go to the beach in her bra and underwear, and she would be arrested for indecent exposure. To my point, it is all about perception. Whether or not you approve of the sexuality in commercials is irrelevant. The point here is perception. However, to that point, how are women perceived in commercials? Recently I saw a TV commercial on ice cream. The woman was wearing a bathing suit supposedly on a beach licking an ice cream cone. Her actions were slow and provocative. How will women be perceived by those watching that commercial? Are they buying the ice cream? IS that a form of exploiting a woman? What do you think?

Many commercials portray women in a provocative sense. I get it, it draws attention to the commercial, the woman is the focus, and the product because of a subliminal thought. For those that may not know what a subliminal thought is, it is a stimulus or mental process that is noticed, by not within the sensation of the conscious mind without being aware of it. However, when you see that product in the store, your mind will make the connection. This is one of the most popular forms of advertising. My point being, if the women are the focus, how are they making the woman be perceived? Do people apply that perception to women as an entire gender? If so, is it reasonable to think that people will feel they have great liberties with women? As I stated earlier, there are many underlying causes. Some may have contributed to some of the female abuse problems we have today, and I emphasize may have. The old saying, *perception perceived is perception achieved*, is very true. *I never have to hit you. I only have to make you believe I would.* I present this question. Over time, have people made women be perceived as a sex object? If so, that could lead to very serious consequences.

In closing this chapter, remember. For every action we take, there is a response. For everything we do, there are consequences. Big things only become big because of the smaller things that got them there.

CHAPTER 11

WHAT DOES THIS ALL MEAN?

We have a female abuse problem that is growing every year, a problem that will not get better without change. I don't' claim to have the answers. That is not what this book is about. I wrote this book to bring awareness, and hopefully suggest ways to prevent it, and tell true stories of those people that have experienced this first hand. You may know people, family, friends, or yourself that have experienced female abuse first hand. This topic is dear to every firefighter, police officer, and EMS personnel that sees it, and lives it each day. I am no better than they are. The difference is I have chosen to write about it in a real and true sense, not in the medical or statistical sense that would have made you through this book in the trash. The stories I have to tell are not over, and the most touching one of all is still yet to come. Two types of woman attend these support groups. There are those that need help, and those that have gotten past it, and want to help others. There is no in-between or grey area. These groups can get quite emotional. The women who have become hardened to their experience can be quite rough on those trying to get through it. There is a fine line as to when sympathy has to stop, and reality needs to set in. Start it too soon, and you lose that person, start it too late, and you might not get them back. These women and counselors are amazing.

Think of your most painful memory or experience. Now think about what it would be like to have to relive it in your mind each day, and often times, many times a day. After an event such as this, it follows the same pattern as with any other traumatic event. GRIEF. Grief has five stages.

1. **Denial** - the stage where we deny to ourselves that is happened. We believe nothing has any value anymore. This stage is a temporary response. However, the length of time varies from person to person depending on other factors such as what the event was.

2. **Anger** - As the grief progress progresses, it turns into anger. You are angry about what happened to you, or what you have lost. This anger can be directed at anyone, including family and friends. You may place blame on someone. Why weren't they there to protect you, why did God let this happen. Blame and anger can manifest itself in many ways.

3. **Bargaining** – You attempt to bargain. Many ask God if he fixes this, they will do something in return, or if I left 2 minutes earlier or later.

4. **Depression** – Then a person enters the depression stage. Reality has set in. You may withdraw from life, your family, or your friends. You might feel as if you are in a fog. You have not energy, no motivation, or desire to move on. In this stage, many people will have suicidal thoughts. This is a very vulnerable stage.

5. **Acceptance** - This is the last stage of grief. Not in the sense that it is okay that something happened, but you have accepted what has happened and you know you are going to be okay. You will survive. You begin to re-enter reality. You accept that this is your new reality, what you have to

live with. You know it was not a good thing, but you know you can live with it.

Everyone will be affected differently through each stage. There is no formula for the length of time. A good support system and positive actions and thinking would certainly reduce the time someone grieves. Some women do not go through this process, or it might be so minimal, they do not realize it. People confuse this will someone being weaker or stronger. That is not the case. What cause this is a person degree of acceptance. Some women can accept what happened, adjust, and move on. Others cannot. No one knows for sure how he or she will react to anything until they are faced with it. Each occurrence in life is different and has a different impact on a person. Just because someone is able to accept some things, that does not mean they will be able to accept everything.

I mentioned that domestic violence is the number cause of female abuse. A woman does not go on a date and be punched in the face on the first date. Domestic violence usually develops in intensity and frequency over time. There are times it may be minor, and the signs of it getting worse are not even noticed as people date over a longer period. Also, if a woman already has self-esteem issues, she may put it with it rather than walking away. 1 in every 4 women will experience some form of domestic violence during her lifetime, with the age range of 20 to 24 being at the greatest risk. A real fact is, every year, 1 in 3 woman who is a victim of homicide is murdered by her current or former partner. Domestic violence affects every aspect of your life, and the sad part is, the vast majority of cases are never reported. Domestic violence is not limited to the heterosexual community. It also exists in same-sex relationships. Let me recap some of the signs to look for. **Once again the toll-free hotline should you need to speak to an advocate is 1-866-223-1111.**

If your partner displays any of the following, you should be concerned:

- Does your partner threaten to hurt you or other people you care about?
- Is there use physical force against you such as, hitting, kicking, pushing, or choking?
- Criticize or blame you for everything that goes wrong?
- Does your partner humiliate you in front of other people?
- Does your partner want to control your access to money?
- Does your partner want to control the decision-making in your relationship?
- Does your partner want to control your time and actions?
- Insult you, put you down, call you names, or make you feel like you're crazy?
- Destroy your property or abuse your pets?
- Does your partner threaten to hurt you or commit suicide if you leave?
- Force or coerce you to have sex when you do not want to?

Let us not confuse some of these examples with what I call a normal disagreement, which all couples have. In an argument, sometimes there is some name-calling. People always want to have the last word or hurt the other. In your household, you may have agreed that one person pays the bills, or controls the money requiring both parties to talk about what they spend their money on. You will be able to determine what is normal for you and what is not. Many times, you may notice other changes before any of the things on the list occur. Things such as:

- Receiving phone calls at weird hours, or leaving the room when they receive a call,
- A change in someone's appearance,
- A change in routine,
- Going out at strange hours,
- Lack of interest.

These are simple things to look for. They could be signs of worst things to come. Many times, especially if both parties work a lot, or are busy with the kids, some of these items are not noticed. No one is suggesting that every move your partner makes be dissected. It is about awareness. When your partners behavior changes, there is a reason for it. If you choose to investigate that reason, talk about it. Do not be confrontational or make unfounded accusations. Trust is like a disease. Once any hint of mistrust is there, it manifests and multiplies as time goes by. So much so, that a person could think they see things that are not there.

A woman was telling her story about a minor domestic abuse situation. In this case, it was the reverse. She was verbally abusing her husband. He was not the type to work out and suddenly joined a gym. He would go there after work, and at times in the morning before work, or on a Saturday morning. When she asked him why he stated he wanted to get in better shape. She went on to say not much else in their relationship changed, except for this. After he was going for a while, she stated they were not having sex as much. When she confronted him, he stated he was just more tired now since he was getting up earlier or coming home later. She did not believe him and started to hound him about constantly. She admitted she was the jealous type. Finally, he was beginning to get angry about all the questions. She asked him to stop going, and he refused. There was some name calling during their arguments, but he never hit her. Finally, she thought she would play it smart and follow him, or sit outside the gym and watch to see if he was there, or meeting anyone. She freely admitted she became obsessed with this. Getting to work late, or leaving early. It was now affecting her job. He also noticed the drop in income. She would tell him work was slow and they let people leave early.

The longer we do things, the easier it is to be caught because we get comfortable with it and drop our guard. Eventually, he caught her in the parking lot. There was a huge argument, and the police were called. He moved out to stay with his brother for a while. During this time, she stalked him. He knew she was, but the reality was, he was not doing anything and had nothing to hide. He spoke to his children every night and saw them on the weekend. Eventually, she insisted they meet to talk. She was convinced he was having an affair. However, this was a thought she escalated in her own mind. He agreed to move home if she went for counseling because he could not take her jealousy any longer. This was why she was there. This was a simple and interesting story. Much less traumatic than what others in the group experienced.

Nevertheless, to this woman, I am sure it was just as impactful. Domestic violence does not always have to involve physical encounters. Emotional abuse can be damaging as well.

Another issue with domestic violence is that many women are in denial that it exists, especially when it comes to emotional abuse. They may leave, but most come back. After all the promises that it will not happen again, the talking, and what a woman believes is a resolution, they return. A woman will leave an unstable relationship an average of seven times before they leave for good. Unstable is defined as any form of domestic violence, especially emotional abuse, which comes in many forms. A woman is with a partner that says what they want but never shows the effort. Always says they will do better. A woman believes the excuses. Eventually, she becomes tired of the excuses and leaves. However, if more promises are made, they will come back, every time. That is the purest example of low self-respect and self-esteem. Most times this is a result of a past relationship or many past relationships. This had now become her normal learned behavior. It is like the woman having an affair with a married man who has promised to leave his wife. Five years later, he is still making the same promise. People fall into traps for a variety of reasons. Low self-respect, esteem, or self-worth share the number one spot. They have most likely suffered from these traits for years. It hurts them on a daily basis. It is as destructive to them as physical violence is to someone else. Keep in mind it is personal, personal to that individual. Over time, the product is an insecure woman. The deeper the feelings of insecurity, the harder it becomes to take action. An action that very well may be what is best for them and lead to a positive outcome. They spend their time making excuses, rather than coming up with solutions. The interesting part is, they know this. They do not face it. The face it means change. Changing what they know. I almost every story I have heard, or every patient I have cared for, each makes the same similar statement. "I knew I should have left sooner," or, "I know what I have to do." Yet, they fail to do it. They are trapped within their own insecurity, which is based on fear.

Many people can function on their own, and many cannot. They need to be with someone, even it that situation is volatile. Think back to how many times you thought to yourself, or said to a friend, "If it were me, I would have left a long time ago. I would never take that shit from anyone." There are varying degrees of sexual abuse. Honestly, when you look at the larger picture, most are minor. Meaning, they do not include violence or physical harm. They are more related to emotional abuse. How many times have you spoken to a friend who has said, "I can't remember the last time I had an orgasm. My husband gets off, rolls over, and goes to bed." That is a form of emotional, sexual abuse resulting from a selfish act of another. I know women that have lived with this for years. My thoughts are, why did they not say something when it started? If it is allowed to continue, that part will become what is considered normal. As I stated earlier, most cases of any form of abuse did not happen overnight, it develops over time. I am not professing that this is the end-all cure to resolve these issues. That would be a completely ignorant statement to make since there are so many other factors, however, with early intervention, many forms of emotional abuse can be worked out.

Life is similar to a picture. A picture is a representation of many smaller elements. Life is the same. Your life as a whole is the big picture. However, the smaller aspects of your life are the individual scenes that comprise the larger picture. Therefore, if you change the scene, you have changed the picture. A woman was telling her story about verbal abuse in her marriage. When her husband was not mad about something and calling her names, or complaining about her, they had a great marriage. She put up with this for many years because she did not want to cause other problems in her marriage. What exactly is that? Is it fear, an excuse, or had she simply become used to it, and accepted that behavior? It was probably a little of both. The group leader handled this very well. She asked, "Why are you here?" The woman replied, "I wanted to see if anyone else was experiencing this same type of problem." We must realize two things. First, to solve any problem, you must admit to yourself there is one. Second, you must want to institute change. The answer could have been easily found out on the internet by looking at studies. With the proper guidance, she eventually admitted she was there to find out how to get help for this problem.

Earlier, we discussed the word embarrassment. People find these topics embarrassing to discuss, especially in a group setting. They feel they are the only ones experiencing this and everyone else has the perfect life or relationship. Embarrassment is like pride. It is hard to swallow. We also discussed that under the main underlying problem or other smaller underlying problems. This is a perfect example of that concept. The first step in resolving anything is taking it down to basics. You must indemnify and face the underlying problems. Many times fixing the underlying problem will repair, or at least take you to the next step to resolve the situation. However, it must start sooner than later. The longer it takes, the more underlying problems develop, therefore, making it harder to address them before you reach a point where you become completely overwhelmed. Does this all sound complicated? If it does, do not let it be. It is quite simple. When you have an issue with something, address it, and fix it, before it becomes habitual.

Another phrase I have heard so many times is, "I just figured he had no one else to take his frustration out on." Does this mean you should be someone's emotional doll? They're go-to person for sex when they need to relieve stress. Should your feelings and emotions be discounted? Domestic violence is much different from a sexual assault case. Domestic violence is imitated by someone you know, and most times, love. A sexual assault is most commonly imitated by a complete stranger. However, in either case, it is not acceptable, so do not make excuses for it. It is human nature for people to "take out," or treat, the people they love the worst. The saying we hurt the ones we love is very true. Mostly because that person feels the other will understand. That is a poor excuse for inappropriate behavior and certainly does not hold water. What this means is somewhere, someone or something is broken. It was either never addressed, causing it to get out of control, or it is a result of multiple different behavioral problems, possibly on the part of both people. Sometimes ignoring a problem make a person partially, or equally as responsible for its outcome. One last topic to discuss before we move to the final chapter is,

"INVOLVEMENT." By this I mean, what is your involvement. Everyone is human, and in the beginning, until things get to the point that they might become physical, fear is not as paramount as defending yourself and striking back. How does this occur?

- Are you yelling just as loud as the other person is?
- Are you calling them names as well?
- Are you adding fuel to the fire?
- Are you helping to escalate the situation?
- Are you enabling this to occur?

In arguments, the first line of defense is an offense. At first, this is how it starts. One person says something, and the other becomes defensive and strikes back. Does this mean you are wrong, of course not? You are only human. What it does mean that in many cases, over time, this can escalate and it can become physical. No one thinks of that possibility because let us be honest. No one ever thinks it will happen to them. Part of the preventive steps is not to engage in this type of action or enable someone else to do this by allowing yourself to be treated in such as manner. This speaks to my statement of a major problem being composed of other underlying problems. In many stories, I have heard, or been total in an ambulance, the phrase, "He just snapped and went off," and, "we have argued so many times it never came to this."

As you can see this is a complex subject that has many variables. Frankly, no one ever thinks about these things. Review the signs I mentioned earlier. This is one. Over time, arguments will become more frequent. As they increase in frequency, the intensity of the arguments can increase as well, until one day, it becomes an explosion. An ounce of prevention is worth a pound of cure. The sad part is, there are times no matter what you do, this cannot be avoided because someone is, who they are. These cases are also more frequent in further relationships. Ask yourself, have you ever spoken to the divorced spouse of the person you are with? Unless people knew each other, that rarely if ever occurs. This could be part of someone's history, and you never knew it. Much of what you learn about your partner should have been found out prior, however, in today's society, people move in together or get married much sooner into a relationship than in years past. The saying, you never really know someone until you live with them is true. However, you can get a very good idea of who and what they are before providing you spend time together and experience different situations together. As with everything else, do not take this chapter to the extremes. An occasional argument does not mean you will be a victim of domestic violence. A healthy exchange of words can be good. It does provide people with a method of relieving some stress and making their concerns and position known if the exchange is a healthy one.

An unhealthy argument can spiral down quickly because there is never really an end goal. It an argument has gotten out of hand and turns into a never-ending argument. It can go on for days and reoccur many times. There are many ways to avoid this. What is paramount to both is what resolution you are trying to come to. Do not let the conversation get out of control. At the first sign of it getting off track, end it, or refocus the conversation to stay on the topic. You can always discuss it later when you are both less emotional. There is no shame if you cannot figure it out to seek outside assistance. It is easier than the possible alternatives. Compromise is always the best solution. Know up front when you meet someone what to look for. Can they compromise, or does everything have to be their way? Everything we are speaking about in this chapter refers to what this all means. Understanding a problem is the key element in solving it. This is assuming we are not dealing with someone that has underlying emotional disorders such as anger management issues. Often times, a woman will know this about her partner when she enters the relationship. That does create a higher risk. However, if they are medicated and controlled, making sure they stay compliant with their medications is important. Any behavioral changes require immediate professional evaluation.

Also, these personality changes can be a result of recent trauma. Some examples could be;

- Someone from the military returning home from overseas duty,

- The recent death of someone close to them
- Loss of a job,
- A result of a constant stressful job,
- Financial problems

These are just a few. The key factor to remember is, not everyone handles things the same way or processes information the same way. These sudden changes in behavior need to be address quickly if they are going to be resolved before they start spiraling downward. We hear this when people are interviewed on the news. Statements such as, "I have lived next to him for years. He was always friendly and seemed like such a nice person." Sometimes these changes are drastic, and sometimes they occur over time. As I mentioned earlier, in some cases they are so subtle, they are not noticed until they become an issue. When I refer back to a previous point that usually means it is an important point. Something you want to remember. The same applies to children. There are cases of child sexual abuse that goes unnoticed.

This book would not be complete if we did not discuss children. Also, an abuse problem that not only affects the child but the parents as well. When a younger child avoids someone, we do not see that as being abnormal if they do not see them often. However, we are not referring to children at three or four years of age. That does not mean that sexual abuse does not happen that young, it does. It is harder to determine because of the social development of a child at those earlier ages. When a child gets older, eight years of age or older, just as an example, when they display fear or reluctance to go to a family member, that should raise a red flag. That does not mean you make blind accusations, it means you become aware, CAREFULLY talk to your child, and if necessary get help. Not all children who fear family members mean they are sexually abused. Sometimes it can be as simple as the child does not like the way the look. Something they may have done in the past scared them, and they remember it. Let me provide you with some information. There are six stages of child development.

1. Newborn – ranges from birth to one month old,
2. Infant development – from one month to one-year-old,

3. Toddler Development – Between one and three years old,
4. Preschool Development – Between three years and five years of age,
5. School-Age Development – Between six and twelve years of age,
6. Adolescent Development – Between 13 and 19 years of age.

Newborn – During this time movements are automatic in response to a stimulus, such as tickling, lightly rubbing your finger on their cheek to induce a smile.

Infant Development – The child starts to exhibit new developmental abilities. They begin to develop better motor control such as controlling their own head movements. They will begin to speak, although usually babble. Some may start to crawl in the later months, and most will respond to things they see or often hear, such as their name.

Toddler Development – They now start to get into routines, such as going to bed at a specific time. They can walk without help but are usually clumsy. They will draw or color, although they may not stay in the lines. The will start to follow simple directions.

Preschool Development - They are now refining their motor skills. Their drawings are more accurate, their balance improves. They are now dressing themselves and are usually using the bathroom. They can engage in longer conversations.

School-Age Development – They are more independent and responsible. They have much better motor skills and begin to develop secondary sexual characteristics. They begin to develop friendships, although they are typically with members of the same sex.

Adolescent Development - During these years, physical, mental, cognitive, and sexual changes occur. The old saying girls mature faster than boys is true. Girls will physically start to mature faster than boys. In their teenage years, they start to develop their opinions and identities, which will get develop further as they get older. They are concerned about their looks. Eating disorders are common during this time. Interests in the opposite sex develop. These are the years they will start to, and what to, spend more time with their friends than their parents.

Genetic makeup determines how early, quickly, and extensively their bodies will develop. Here is a fact you should know. As high as 93% of victims under the age of 18 know the person who abused them. You usually do not have to look that far. There are many warning signs of child sexual abuse. Rainn.org is a great place to view these.

- Bleeding, bruises, or swelling in the genital area
- Bloody, torn, or stained underclothes
- Difficulty walking or sitting
- Frequent urinary or yeast infections
- Pain, itching, or burning in the genital area

WATCH FOR BEHAVIORAL SIGNS: *(courtesy of rainn.org)*

- Changes in hygiene, such as refusing to bathe or bathing excessively
- Develops phobias
- Exhibits signs of depression or post-traumatic stress disorder
- Expresses suicidal thoughts, especially in adolescents
- Has trouble in school, such as absences or drops in grades
- Inappropriate sexual knowledge or behaviors
- Nightmares or bed-wetting
- Overly protective and concerned for siblings, or assumes a caretaker role
- Returns to regressive behaviors, such as thumb sucking
- Runs away from home or school
- Self-harm
- Shrinks away or seems threatened by physical contact

TOLL-FREE HELP NUMBER – 1-800-422-4453

I wanted to provide information on children because this is also a very important topic and female abuse or male abuse is NOT limited to a specific age group. This book would not be complete if children were not discussed. One experience I had before we move on to the final chapter.

Child abuse problems also include these such as child sex trafficking. According to an article published in February of 2017, The HuffPost states, according to UICEF, every two minutes a child is being prepared for sexual exploitation. 1.2 million Children alone are being trafficked every year. This number does not reflect those that have already been held captive by trafficking. It is estimated that 30 million children have lost their childhood through sexual exploitation over the past 30 years. People are trafficked from 127 countries and are exploited in 137 countries according to the United Nations. They are used as prostitutes, house cleaners, and servants. Some as young as nine years old, and even sadder, many of these girls contract HIV within two years, and many die before reaching the age of 20. Many parents never find out what happened to their children. This is another example of a life-altering experience. Many parents are never the same after an abduction. Many of these girls ran away from home for various reasons. Sometimes those reasons are related to parental sexual abuse. They wind up in a far worse place. This relates back to reporting. The child is afraid to tell anyone.

Should this reporting process be explained to children? Should they have the information and feel safe reporting something to the other parent, or parents if it is a family member involved? Children are delicate but are much stronger than parents or people give them credit for. In the case of children, it is not what you say or explain to them, it is more related to how you do it. Parents should seek advice on this matter from their pediatrician. Should this topic be discussed in a classroom setting when children reach a certain age? Let me ask you another question. In school, if we are going to teach children about sex, and how to protect themselves, why shouldn't we explain everything? Teach them, educate them, and help to protect them even more? These are all things I am presenting to you to consider. My children are all grown and on their own. I thank God each day that they had a normal childhood and did not have to suffer from these issues, however, as a father, I explained and taught them about these issues. In a manner, they could understand. Their mother and I discussed this first and decided any piece of fear that might have developed, if explained properly, was worth saving them from becoming a statistic. Of course, these are your decisions. I will not give advice on any of the questions I proposed to you. However, I can and did tell you how as a parent, I handled it.

I said this a couple of times in this book. I am not a doctor. Therefore, I do not give advice. However, I am educated with over 30 years of real-life experience and have spoken with hundreds of victims over the years. All of this combined, along with the true stories, which are only the tip of the iceberg of what I have seen, and my experience, validate every written word in this book. It is a sad way to learn all of this, but they are real, true, and witnessed. I am sure I have presented many things in this book that many of you reading it had no idea existed on the scale that is does. That is called awareness. However, whether you choose to act on it or not, is your choice. All I can do is present you with the information, which includes the hard cold facts. The ones that will make you cry, make you feel some fear, and hopefully cause you to react. I will bet that some parents that read this section are getting up to go check on their child sleeping in bed. One of the most difficult realities I had to face in my life was having young children growing up while I had to care for those that were victims. It took time for me to get a handle on balancing the two. Here is a short off the topic story. See if you get the underlying message.

I must remind everyone, that ages, names or locations of events, or stories, are NOT divulged. This is a very sensitive topic, and privacy is of the utmost concern. I have worked as a paramedic in numerous cities, actually in the hundreds, some while visiting or working in other states. I will not provide any information that could jeopardize the privacy of any individual.

I responded to a call for a young girl that was struck by a truck while riding her bike. As we approached the accident scene, we could see the skin that scraped off her body on the road. When we arrived, we found a young girl wedged between the road, her bicycle, and the fender of the truck. I expected to find her dead. Thanks to God, she was alive. We had to get her out. The fire department arrived just as we did. They deployed their airbag lift to raise the front of the truck. When we got her out, the left side of her chest was scraped clean, almost to the bone. She had a broken leg, and multiple cuts and bruises. She was in shock and could not react to the pain she was feeling, which I can guarantee was tremendous. We did what is known as "scoop and run." Perform as much treatment you could while transporting the patient to the hospital. What they need most is a trauma room or possibly surgery. Our job is to keep them alive and get them there. You do not waste time at the scene. I know I am being critical when I say this, but as an educator of paramedics for 20 years, I have earned the right to say, a paramedic is worthless if they cannot do their job in a moving ambulance. Many times, that is the place where life or death will occur.

I gave a quick notification to the pediatric emergency department and told them how long it would take us to get there. I would be to busy to give any further updates. I knew they would a full trauma team waiting when we arrived. Her heart rate was slow, and her blood pressure was dangerously low. Children are different from adults. They will remain stable longer but crash quickly, right before your eyes. When they do, you have lost them. I was not going to lose this little girl. With the help of the fire department paramedic who assisted in, we established two access points in her veins, called IV's, was managing her breathing, and we stabilized her as we got to the emergency room. They did the rest. The total time of this call from dispatch to arrival at the scene and arrival at the emergency room was 22 minutes. She survived; not by my hands, but by the hand of God. He gave me the tools to be good at my job. Being scientifically minded, every field person has a special relationship between themselves and God. Regardless of your beliefs, I cannot count how many times during a call I asked God to help me save someone. In the many cases when you thought there was no hope, and you are working with a bloody tangled body, you asked God to help you find a way. This little girl survived and would face many years of continued reconstructive surgery to rebuild what was left on the asphalt. It was not the trucks fault. She came out between two cars, he never saw her. She was too small. He only knew he hit something because he felt that the front end of the truck was not right. He stopped to check it. If he had kept going, she would have died. Even knowing that the accident was not ruled the driver's fault; can you imagine what he has to emotionally live with? Let's continue.

Most do not understand what goes into being a health care provider. Whether you are a basic level EMT, and advance provider as a Paramedic, a Doctor, Nurse, Technician, or anyone else that works in the healthcare field. You do not understand it because you do not do it for a living. Therefore, your knowledge is limited to what you see or hear on the news, or from those you may know who work in the field. The things that are seen can be horrific, emotional, and life-altering. Many providers cannot do this job for long; others take their own life, while others find a coping mechanism. I was one of the lucky ones. I loved what I did so much I was able to find a coping mechanism and gave it 30+ years of my life. That did not come without much heartache and asking myself many questions along the way. However, I had the honor and privilege to help and service others. If I had to do it all over, I would not change a thing. It helped make me a better man and person, and most importantly, a good father. It gave as much to me as I gave in return.

I was involved in a case that involved two children. I will not discuss the details other than to say, a parent called because of some marks found on the children. They were cared for, and the marks were suspicious enough that an investigation was started. It was found out that someone who cared for these children not only abused them but had them abuse each other. Remember, abuse is a wide term that is not limited to penetration. We have all seen the news stories of a young child that was raped by an adult. These are horrific events, and no one can get their head around them. We are thankful that it has not happened to our children. However, it does happen to other children. Therefore, you cannot ignore it. Every parent needs to be pro-active with whom they place the care of their child.

CHAPTER 12

FACING REALITY

We have faced a great deal of truth and reality in this book, as well as data, statistics, and true stories. It is real. Everything discussed in this book validates not only myself as a writer but the subject. Anyone could certainly choose to ignore it, I cannot. I have seen too much of this reality, and have had friends that were victims of it in one respect or another. I should not be ignored. I am not the only Paramedic in the world that has been witness to these many tragedies. I commend all my colleagues and those studying to enter this field of medicine. It will challenge you in every way imaginable. My only advice to you is what those who taught me said. "Never forget what you signed up to do."

Facing reality is never easy. In the case of female abuse, it comes with a great deal of pain and suffering. If you are a victim, or a past victim, you must believe some people want to help you. As alone as you may feel, you are not alone. Being or feeling alone is a state of mind, not always a physical state. At times, we feel as though we cannot control our emotions or thoughts. Our imaginations as "what if" scenarios run rampant in our minds. Controlling your mind and your thoughts takes a great deal of practice. Finding that place in your mind that brings you to peace is even harder. Everything in life comes with a price. However, you can pay the price when you face reality, accept it, and take the necessary steps to move past it. Besides what we learn in school, the most valuable lessons are what we learn in life. Education cannot provide you with courage, tenacity, and real-life experience. It can provide you with the knowledge to understand. The rest is what living life does. It fills in the gaps between academic knowledge and life. Many do live with one or the other, and many live with both. To achieve the most fulfilling life you can, you need both. You cannot be afraid to live; you only need the ability of knowledge to be able to live a less fearful life. Prevent the unthinkable, and if faced with it, survive. If you are reading this book and are a past victim of female abuse, you survived. If you are not or have never been a victim, possibly this book will help you to survive, or never become a victim at all.

Reality is one of the most feared things in our society. We do not want to face it, realize this shit does happen, or it threatens the existence we know. Closing your windows to drown out the screams of your neighbor's wife, so you do not hear them, does not mean the problem went away. It means you just choose not to accept it, but it still exists. Some people can live that life. I cannot. Each person has a different degree of strength. I will not judge those that close their windows. I can say I do not agree with it, but I will not judge them. Everyone must know his or her own limitations. The fear of people not wanting to get involved is real. No one should put his or her eggs in one basket and rely on the fact that someone will intervene. They may, or they may not. It is your responsibility to do whatever you can to be sure the situation does not exist in the first place. You can only do that by facing reality. Thankfully, in many respects, people, are becoming more involved with helping others. They are taking the risk to do the right thing when someone needs help.

A quick story off topic for a moment, because it refers to reality. One day while sitting in our ambulance at a light in a downtown area of the town we were covering, we noticed an elderly female walking down the sidewalk with a small bags holder. Her pocketbook was draped over her head and across a shoulder. This is a common way to carry a pocketbook so someone cannot slip it off your hand or grab it from your hands. It was a Saturday afternoon, so the sidewalks had people on them. Two young men were approaching the elderly woman from behind. My partner and I noticed them. Things developed very quickly. They ran up to her and tried to pull her pocketbook away. She fought back. It was not easy getting the pocketbook away. I said to my partner call have dispatch call the police and I left the ambulance and started to run across the street to help her., As I was running, I could not help but notice NO ONE was assisting her. I remember saying to myself, "What the hell is wrong with these people." When I approached, I place one in a headlock so I could see where the other was, as he started to approach me to help his friend, my partner arrived and took him to the ground. We held them, and seconds later two police cruisers arrived and took them into custody. Our dispatcher sent a second ambulance to assist us in the event the police were further away. They were checking the woman for injuries and thankfully, she was fine, but a bit shook up. While we were giving our statements to the police, the woman came over to thank us. As it turned out, she had 1.45 cents left in her wallet after shopping.

The moral of this story is not what we did. Although not within the realm of our job description, it was the right thing to do. The moral is, so many people were just watching and doing nothing. Could they have had a knife, gun, or another weapon? That thought never crossed our minds. For many, it does. They choose not to get involved so as not to run the risk of getting hurt, or ramifications later. The police have great response times, but that depends on where they are coming from, or how busy they are. Most people do not realize that, so they choose to do nothing and wait for the police. Medical personnel do not carry weapons. That is strictly forbidden. However, since they run the risk of being assaulted, or worse, they are trained with some basic self-defense procedures. Is it a dangerous job, you bet it is? I have brought an ambulance back to the garage with bullet holes in it from being shot out. I have been assaulted my more than one person at the same time, I had been attacked with a knife, and ax, and once a machete. I have had a few job-related surgeries due to injuries sustained, and have broken my share of bones. Some make it through their entire career with no injuries. Others are not as fortunate. You accept that reality, and you move on. This is an example of reality regarding what I was discussing. The key is to control your fears, and not have them control you. When fear controls you, you make mistakes, bad judgment calls, and are very vulnerable. Fear in itself is healthy when embraced. As a retired firefighter, I can tell you that every firefighter has a certain degree of fear when they enter a burning building. However, we are trained to use that fear to our advantage; to allow it to make us smarter. We train every day for every possible scenario. That is how we control our fear. When faced with that fear, our training takes over, and our fear is overcome. We can do our jobs effectively. Police, military, or other services operate under the same principles.

The reality of female abuse can also operate under those same parameters if you face reality and are prepared for it. In your case, your preparation is accomplished through awareness and prevention, along with the knowledge this book has provided you with. Earlier I gave you some data on women murdered by an ex-boyfriend or husband. I must ask myself as you should ask yourself. Why would any person that left a highly volatile situation put himself or herself in a position to be alone with that person, or let them into their home? Is that a good example of prevention? Some decisions in life we make, we must think two steps ahead of it before we make it. I use this as an example because there was a case where an ugly divorce occurred. The parties involved were in an explosive situation throughout the divorce. This one made national news so you might be aware of it. The wife started to date. The ex-husband called her one night and asked if he could come over to talk. He came over, and she let him in. He killed her, and then himself. What could have possibly avoided this tragedy? Awareness, meaning, being aware of the explosive nature of their relationship, and insist on phone calls rather than a visit. Many times after a divorce, the wounds for one or the other are fresh. It takes time for them to heal. If someone is mentally unstable, it takes even longer, or may not totally heal. I am NOT advocating that every divorced man is going to kill his wife, so do not take this story out of the content it was intended. I am simply stating that being aware is part of facing reality.

When we are prepared, we are not preparing for what is going to happen, because we do not know that. What we are preparing for is the possibility. The same as why you save money. You do not know when or if your furnace will break, but you become prepared financially in case it does. If you look at everything in life as it happens, you will never leave your house, let alone live your life. My father used to say, "Prepare for the worst, and hope for the best." This is how we all deal with reality, or how we all should. Reality is the world or the state of things, as they ACTUALLY exist, as opposed to an idealistic or notional idea of them. With that said, people can perceive reality differently, make reality what they want it to, or hope it to be. That is idealism, not reality. It gives an individual a false sense of security. Keep in mind that most things do not happen when you expect them to. They happen when you least expect them. I get it. This is a scary book to read, and it should be. Any self-help book that deals with the many tragic events that can occur, and have occurred, can have that effect. However, they are educational, and as I stated previously, the key is awareness and [prevention. They are not educational in the academic sense where you take a test and need to pass it, it is educational in the life sense. Before getting into the fire service and working in pre-hospital medicine, I never knew half of what I saw existed in the world. I always tell people you do not need to fear what you hear about on the news. You need to fear the things you never hear about on the news. What you hear about you are educated to. What you do not hear about, you have no clue it exists. Trust me, it does.

In everyone's life, they experience something, or something happens that has a great impact on their life. Soon, you will hear the story that made this topic so special to me some time ago. I vividly remember every call that touched my heart in one way or another. However, the story I will soon tell you is the one that had the most impact on me in my entire career. I first want to wrap up a couple of more closing remarks. For the women reading this book, you do not give yourself enough credit when it comes to your strength. Sit back and think for a moment. Think about how much you do, and how much you accomplish. How much input you have in holding things together when times are difficult. These are all examples of your strength. Strength is not about how much weight you can lift in the gym, strength is about your heart, your mind, and your soul. It is what gives you the perseverance to overcome obstacles. A humorous statement a woman once said to me, as it is true. ***"If I could passing a baby the size of a football between my*** *legs, I can do anything."* The interesting part about strength is that no one ever really knows how strong they are until they are put to the task. Isn't this what we have tried to prepare for ourselves for our entire life without even realizing it? By life's experiences alone, some will be stronger than others will. This is another reality. This is why I say, you can never judge another by using yourself or anyone else as a comparison. With the younger generation now cohabitating, things have changed. Men take more of a role in helping then generations past. However, the majority of the burden in the household, especially one with children, sits in the hands of the woman. The phrase, "A man buys a house, but the woman makes it a home is true." Do not underestimate your strength.

The last topic I want to discuss regarding A Woman's Fear is her emotions. As a reminder, when I use the word "MOST," it refers to the population in general, not a specific person. Since the beginning of time, history has taught us that woman have been abused in a variety of ways. Even though things have improved, we still live a three-generation multi-cultural society. Through attrition alone, things will become better for women, and hopefully, these types of event will decrease as old school thinking goes away. However, DNA makeup takes generations to change. Therefore, some principals will outlive us all for some time. Men are physical, and women are emotional. Most men do not have to feel any emotions to have intimate relations with a woman. It is a physical desire, driven by a different set of needs based on their hormones. However, most women have to at least like their sexual partner or feel a sense of emotional attraction to them. This is a generalized fact. There are certainly exceptions is both genders.

There are also different thought processes. If most women discover a man has cheated on them, they feel an emotional and physical betrayal, and may not leave the relationship. However, to most men, if his partner cheats on him, he will be not as tolerable of this. However, if he cheats on her, to him, it means nothing; it was only sex. This topic is discussed in great depth, and I provide amazing data in my book, *"Making Partnership Choices."* In this case, I am using it as an example of the perceptional difference between genders. This does vary in same-sex relationships. Maybe this is why intimate relations between people change over time. Another major difference is a woman will try harder and longer to fix things and be more forgiving due to her emotional baseline. However, she will carry it with her for a long time. Men, on the other hand, will stay, not due to emotions, due to other factors. Finances, child support, or alimony, are the main influencing factors. How's that saying go, "It's cheaper to keep her?" When you tie all these factors together, it is easy to see how the underlying issues add up. They can lead to arguments, which can escalate over time, and lead to various forms of abuse. When you look at your relationship, have you ever broke it down to this detail? Of course, you have not, most do not. People never do until they have a need to. How much tragedy could be avoided with a little bit of knowledge, communications, and desire?

A woman's emotions run deep, and many women hold them in rather than discuss them. In many instances, they wait so long that by the time they discuss, they are a major issue, and the man does not know where any of this is coming from. Part of that is their responsibility because they have not noticed some things that might have changed along the way. Because women hold back their emotions and remember things much longer, it will have a greater effect on them. Even an argument with a girlfriend will emotionally bother them until it is resolved. Personalities, cultures, and upbringing, also play a part in this. The way an individual handles their emotions is important because it is directly related to how a woman will heal from an abusive situation. It helps to explain why some heal faster, others take longer, and some never do. Maybe people take the approach of, "just get some medicine from the doctor." In cases of mental strain, medication does not fix the problem; it only helps with the symptoms. We are not treating an infection. The emotional cure comes from facing the event, talking it out with professionals, or in a controlled group setting. A woman does not understand why this happened to her. You will not fix that with a pill.

As with men, there are hormone changes that change in women as they reach an older age. These will also vary from woman to woman and can manifest in many different ways. Many women avoid thinking about this as they feel these changes and do not discuss them with their partner. This underlying issue can add additional stress. This stress can lead to impatience, and possibly arguments. It can also lead to infidelity in a relationship. Life is ever changing, and not always the way we would prefer. The reverse is for men. Many men can develop erectile dysfunction issues at younger ages than other men. For a man, this is a frustrating time as they suffer from denial, embarrassment, and other symptoms. They do not discuss this with their wife, and often times will blame their wife for lack of performance. They find that easier than admitting they have a problem. A problem, by the way, is easy to fix by consulting their doctor. However, in their eyes, it represents a problem for them when it comes to feeling like a man. This is an example of another underlying problem. Woman are much more understanding of this male problem than the man is of the female problem. In many domestic violence cases, this leads to arguments that develop into some form of abuse. I have heard many stories from women where they defined this as the root of the problem. During this period, some men will seek pleasure elsewhere to see if the problem is at home. At least that is their logic. Once they find that it is not, this further adds to their denial, stress, embarrassment, and lack of patience and tolerance.

As I stated earlier, most domestic violence cases develop over time. The key to repairing them is to find and repair what caused them, providing they had not already reached an unrepairable state. This is why open and honest communications are paramount. People do not spend their day learning about the changes their body will undergo. Yes, women know that at some point, they will enter menopause, and men know that they will develop erectile dysfunction. However, most do not know what comes with those conditions. Therefore, they do not face them as they develop. Men exhibit a great deal of pride. Erectile dysfunction is a true blow to their sense of pride and manhood. As we approach the end of this book, I hope that I have provided you with a sense of truth, reality, and understanding. In my pre-hospital medical career, I have cared for 76,251 patients, delivered thirteen babies, and pronounced more people deceased than I care to think out. Most Paramedics are like snipers. There are things we personal track of. Many choose different things. My education, medical experience, and talking to those who have experienced these type of abuse is what validates this writing. I always choose to keep track of the happier statistics of my career, although I never kept track of the number that died. However, I know the number is quite high and ranges from the age of an infant to elderly adults. Some were by natural causes and many due to traumatic events.

Along with some data, we also have cases that had a great impact on us as people. In my case, there are two calls I will never forget. Earlier I said I would share those stories. They will be graphic. They must be for you to understand.

One rainy night, we were dispatched to cover a call in another town for a motor vehicle accident. The roads were wet. The road was desolate, and it was late. The curve was not sharp, so the car had to be traveling at a high rate of speed. Due to the road conditions, and the fact there was no evidence that the car hit the brakes, by the damage alone, it was estimated the vehicle had to be traveling close to one hundred miles per hour. When we arrived, the fire department was frantically trying to figure out how they would get the occupants out. There were pieces of the car everywhere, and the main body of the car was almost completely crushed and wrapped around a tree. The fire department had their lights set up because it was so dark. When my partner and I exited our unit, the fire department was tending to a young female that was ejected from the car and was up against a tree about thirty feet away. They yelled for me to come over. She was a mess. Most of her face was crushed, and her neck was broken and dangling like a slinky. I pronounced her deceased and started towards the car. Upon looking inside the vehicle, bodies were stacked up. The interior was so mangled; all you could see was one or two heads, some legs, and feet. There were more legs and feet than heads. We knew there were more than two people in the car. The fire department had to stabilize the car. We all knew it would take close to thirty-minutes of extraction time before we got to victims. By that time, if they were not already dead, they probably would be. It was time for a decision.

On a scene such as this, the fire department is in charge. However, the highest-ranking medical person on the scene is in charge of the medical treatment. That person was me. I did not know how many people were in the car, but by the looks the bodies I could see, and the damage, I knew no one could have survived this crash. After a very quick discussion with the fire chief, we decided to make an opening large enough for me to crawl through to evaluate the people in the car. In these situations where there is this much damage, it is easy to cause more harm by making a hasty decision. There were no signs of life. You also need to be concerned about the safety of the personnel on scene. These are not easy decisions. Do you try to get to them and maybe kill someone if anything goes wrong, or do you evaluate? As of that time in my career, I had never seen a car damaged to this degree, and I had seen many. The car was so crushed, there was only about a six-inch opening to see in. Without rapidly cutting this car apart without taking safety precautions, it would take about ten minutes just to make an opening big enough for me. To add more to the story, the gas tank was punctured, and there was gasoline all over. The fire department would have to lay down a layer of foam so any sparks would not ignite the gasoline, especially while I was in the car. The one thing a fire department does best is multi-tasking. They know their jobs. I am not saying that because I was a firefighter, I am saying that because this is why they train so extensively. They prepare for the worst.

Keep in mind the inside of this car has torn metal everywhere. You could easily be cut and suffer a severe bleeding injury during the rescue. Great care must be taken. A firefighter gave me his protective coat and gloves to wear. I entered the vehicle while two firefighters held me by the ankles. I descended into the wreck. The first two patients I checked were the two victims I could get too quickly. Their faces were intact. However, they were both deceased. Probably due to internal injuries, which caused rapid blood loss. Someone was taking notes because an accurate time of death must be recorded. All I could see now were legs and feet. The seats were torn off their mounts. I had to move them around in the vehicle to get to the other occupants. As I did this, I found three more bodies. One head was partially cut off, one was crushed, and the last person's chest was crushed. None of them had any signs of life. The thing about someone who is dead; is they look dead. Almost all the victims still had their eyes open. Some eyes were protruding; others had a blank dead stare. A person with internal injuries so severe that they bleed out internally has no color. I pronounce the last three dead. I exited the vehicle, thanked and returned the coat and gloves to the firefighter, walked over to the side of the road and sat for a moment. My partner that was giving me the equipment I needed along the way went to our unit and cried. This was the most people I had to pronounce dead at one time. I may have had two or even three through a single or double shift, but this was six people dead on one call. Other paramedics have had to pronounce more than that on one scene, especially those in a war zone. I could now imagine what they felt. This was a life changing call for me. One I will never forget. Writing these paragraphs, I could still see their faces.

The call I am about to describe, which is related to this topic, is the call that made this topic so important to me. I have been on countless domestic violence calls. Many that were involved more than an argument or a slap. Situations when physical abuse and violence occurred. I have seen women with their eyes so swollen they could not open them. Teeth were punched out, arms or hands were broken, or jaws were broken, as well as women who sustained multiple cuts and bruises during an altercation, or internal injuries. However, by far, this next call was the worst. The call that made this topic a passion for me, and caused to continue to be involved the even after my medical career ended. I still do a great deal of teaching, but rarely work the road anymore. This was another life-changing call for me.

While working a double shift, we received a call about one and a half hours before the end of our shift. It was to meet the police for a woman found on the side of the road. When we arrived, there were multiple police on the scene, and they had already set up a crime scene perimeter. I can tell you this. That is NEVER a good sign. We exited our vehicle and started to get our equipment when an officer approached and said you will not need that, we just need you to confirm the death. As we walked by the vehicle, a female officer was tending to two children in a car seat. I asked the officer if they were checked. He said one of the other EMT's checked them, and they were fine. Since I was the highest-level care provider on the scene, I needed to and wanted to check them. Child services were on the way, and the father had not been notified. They wanted to wait until the children were at the hospital. They preferred that the father not come to the crime scene. This is another bad sign. There were police and forensic people everywhere. I had to be escorted in and out of the crime scene, and give my full information should any of my DNA show up on the scene. Even one piece of hair that falls out could be found and place someone at a crime scene. They need a full accounting of everyone that is there.

I had a general idea of what I was going to find. No matter how much you do this job, the adrenaline pumps. I could feel my heart rate getting faster as we approached and I saw a body that was covered by a blanket that the police used to cover the body. Thousands of thoughts race through your mind as to what you might see. In an emergency setting, things happen so fast you never have time to think about this. However, after the fact, your mind has that time. You start to prepare yourself for the worse; the medical examiner had not shown up yet. The police needed medical personnel to confirm the death. Before the body was uncovered, I was instructed as to what I could, and could not touch. These crimes scenes are very difficult. I have been to a crime scene where the person was assumed deceased, when in fact, they were alive. You must rapidly care for this patient without disturbing anything. That is quite a challenge. Looking at the blanket, I could see some blood that had soaked into it. I took my position where I felt if the victim were still alive, we could move her without disturbing anything. My partner had our stretcher and equipment at the roadside just in case. Care was taken to be sure no one was around us when the blanket was removed. As the detective uncovered the victim, I wanted to die. What I witnessed next caused so much anger inside of me. A woman was on the ground with no clothes on. Her clothing was next to her body, clearly indicating the probability of a sexual assault. She was brutally beaten and stabbed. That was where the blood on the blanket

came from. I will not describe it any further. She was found by
a passerby who called 911 but was afraid to get out of their car
because they were not on scene when we arrived.

The thoughts immediately ran through my mind. Did the
children witness this? She was found about twenty feet from the car,
it was dark, and she was next to the bushes. I believed, or hoped,
the bushes blocked the view from the car. In a case like this, you
cannot change what has happened. The victim is gone. The new
victims are the husband and the children. I have the greatest respect
for the doctor who would have to tell her husband. I have told many
families members that their loved ones have passed away. This was
not your standard death due to natural causes. After I pronounced
her deceased, I walked away. I did not know if I wanted to cry
or grab the first thing I saw and beat it. I walked over to the car
because I wanted to check on the children. Child service had just
arrived and said that was not necessary, they were already checked.
I said to the agent, please, this is something I have to do. I know
she understood because she let me check the children. My medical
report had to be letter perfect. If the assailants were apprehended,
my medical documentation as to how the body was found would be
evidence in a trial. To write such a detailed report takes a little time.
Time, that while you are writing, you are reliving the entire event.
To survive in this line of work, you MUST be able to find your
peace to cope with all the things you see. Those that cannot either
quit and get into a different line of work such as dispatching or after
some time, might commit suicide.

When we educate the upcoming new providers, we cannot
teach them how to cope. You can give them the tools, but they
must be able to find what works for them. I have seen so many
kill himself or herself, become alcoholics or drug users when they
leave the profession because they could not cope. The moral is,
there are many victims besides those that are directly affected.
My way of coping was not to bury it, run from, or not face it. I
never ran, forgot it, or buried it. What worked for me was sharing.
Teaching others and continuing to help those that needed help.
Talking to groups whenever possible, and seeing the survivors
that were trying to get back to a normal life, or helping others to

do the same. That was my way of coping. That is what worked for me. These experiences made me realize that everything I did, and everything I witnessed, every person I took care of, God presented to me to help me help others, and make me a better person. This book is just one of my ways of doing that.

I will not end this book by saying I hoped you enjoyed it. It is not a topic to enjoy. However, if it touched the life of one person, one person that could avoid a tragedy, I was successful. I would only ask that you leave a review on this book at whatever site you purchased it. Recommend it to your friends. Every woman should be aware of this crucial topic. Yes, even men. Good men should know what bad men do.

In closing, this book is about being thankful. If you are fortunate enough to have that great relationship, never take it for granted, and be thankful for it every day. It is always easier to prevent a problem than it is to correct it. God bless every woman that has had a bad experience. May God speed your healing. I will leave you with this final thought.

Although the world is full of suffering,
it is also full of the overcoming of it.
~ Hellen Keller ~

CREDITS

Book cover design by Jodilocks Designs

1in6.org

Center for Disease Control

CDV.org

Google.com

HuffPost

Livestrong.com

Wikipedia.com

Merriam Webster

Trustify.info

PBS.org

Government statistics

Pmenicanspec.org

Printed in the United States
By Bookmasters